Individualizing
Professional
Development

This book is dedicated to Barbara Rockwell Quinn, my mother, and Barry Richard Husby, my husband. My mother inspires me because she is always willing to improve herself and does so in all sorts of ways, is independent, strong, and endearingly benevolent, is just eccentric enough to be interesting, and because she allowed me the freedom and voice to become somebody almost like her. I am indebted to my husband for his vision. He has always believed me capable of accomplishing much more than I could imagine, and he's never let me settle for just dreaming.

Individualizing Professional Development

A Framework for Meeting School and District Goals

Vicki R. Husby

Foreword by Jo Blase

CORWIN PRESS
A Sage Publications Company
Thousand Oaks, California

For information:

Corwin Press
A Sage Publications Company
2455 Teller Road
Thousand Oaks, California 91320
www.corwinpress.com

Sage Publications Ltd.
1 Oliver's Yard
55 City Road
London EC1Y 1SP
United Kingdom

Sage Publications India Pvt. Ltd.
B-42, Panchsheel Enclave
Post Box 4109
New Delhi 110 017 India

Printed in the United States of America

Library of Congress Cataloging-in-Publication Data

Husby, Vicki R.
Individualizing professional development : a framework for meeting school and district goals / Vicki R. Husby.
        p. cm.
Includes bibliographical references and index.
ISBN 1-4129-0941-4 (cloth) — ISBN 1-4129-0942-2 (pbk.)
   1. Teachers—In-service training—United States. 2. Individualized education programs—United States. 3. School personnel management—United States. I. Title.
LB1731.H33 2005
370'.71'55—dc22

                                                        2004024086

This book is printed on acid-free paper.

05   06   07   08   09   10   9   8   7   6   5   4   3   2   1

Acquisitions Editor:	Rachel Livsey
Editorial Assistant:	Phyllis Cappello
Production Editor:	Kristen Gibson
Copy Editor:	Diana Breti
Typesetter:	C&M Digitals (P) Ltd.
Proofreader:	Kristin Bergstad
Indexer:	Cristina Haley
Cover Designer:	Michael Dubowe
Graphic Designer	Lisa Miller

Contents

List of Tables
and Figures

Foreword

Jo Blase, University of Georgia

BETWEEN PAST AND FUTURE

The recurring crisis in American education, which is now a political problem of the first magnitude, has resulted in educators' work becoming incomparably more complex, challenging, and important than ever before. And, similar to our children's inalienable civic right to an education, American teachers arguably have a right to premier ongoing professional education and development that sharpens their skills and enables them to grow in their ability to address the myriad learning needs of diverse children in today's increasingly demanding educational environment.

Although it has long been an axiomatic assumption that professional growth is a predictable effect of educators' development programs, teachers in this, the most advanced and modern country in the world, are still finding that professional growth opportunities are underdeveloped and, at times, of little or no use. In the midst of what, to some, appears to be a multitude of weak and ill-formed professional development programs, we are still erroneously inclined to believe that teacher development programs automatically translate into expert classroom teaching as soon as staff development sessions end, that we can substitute professional development sessions unrelated to assessment and action research for true teacher development and learning, that age-old contradictions between teachers' needs and wants are inconsequential, that we must uncritically and slavishly accept mediocrity and an astounding hodgepodge of sense and nonsense in professional development programs, that teachers are incapable of facilitating their own professional growth, and that we are everlastingly stuck on the horns of political-economic-social dilemmas when it comes to financing and implementing teacher development programs. One obvious symptom of the estrangement of teachers' professional growth programs from the daily work of education is the chronic overload American teachers suffer, often an overload brought about in part by extraneous work caused by bogus "development" or "improvement" programs. The difficulty can be summed up as a contradiction between our ideal development programs and our everyday experiences, a sad and glaring contradiction for too many American teachers in too many American schools.

In fact, the frightening illusion of widespread weak professional development programs is doubtless stronger than reality, but the destructiveness of our basic assumptions about professional development and our inability to escape the cycle of those poor programs that do exist is obliterating the distinction between wasteful activity and true professional learning, change for change's sake and growth, inactivity and directed action. As common sense disappears, stagnation creeps in and occupies the space meant for human development, and like a dragon lying in wait for hapless teachers trapped in a hopeless enterprise, the whole attempt can become a sort of fraud. We have lost our way, at least in part, and now is the time to replace such pernicious, ruinous programs with programs designed to ensure that teachers' individual learning needs are met. This is a tall order, but in this book, Vicki Husby has methodically and comprehensively filled that order.

Thus we are indeed between past and future. We cannot simply go on in unreflective perseverance, offering feeble and irrelevant staff development programs. The demands of society in the form of accountability and our veritable future are before us. It is now a self-evident truth that we must shed old-world thinking about professional development programs and rebuild our common professional world. We must eliminate the danger of pointless programs and involve teachers in meaningful and productive professional growth. We are brought to the puzzling question of how to do this.

In Husby's book, the first step in creating effective and meaningful new professional development programs, that of "seal[ing] the proverbial crack in contemporary professional development of educators," is a fait accompli. Developed around an unassailable conceptual framework of adult learning theory, self-directed learning wherein learner control is significant, action research on the effectiveness of practices and programs, critical reflection on ingrained beliefs in order to transform and grow, and group learning in trusting environments (hence, the development of a professional learning community), Husby pointedly addresses the interests and standards of society; her individualized professional development program provides for professional accountability because individuals' goals must impact student achievement, and it adheres to professional standards as explicated by the National Staff Development Council.

Refreshingly, Husby trusts in the infinite perfectibility of professional performance as she insists that individual focus areas in self-directed professional development programs must relate to professional responsibilities, align with school and district goals, and impact student achievement. Learning modes for teachers in the program include self-instruction, cooperative learning, and team learning, and flexible methods and time frames are embraced. Features include step-by-step directions for developing the program, agendas for implementation, materials for mini-lessons, examples of learning plans, materials for use within reform model professional development programs, and a revealing collection of teacher comments in response to the program. Structural concerns and facilitator behaviors are addressed in an accessible do/do not format.

Husby also captures and defines a space wherein American teachers can pursue this vital development together. In this space, "a venture to empower adults to develop themselves," teachers have a right to speak and be heard. In this space, dialogue between and among fellow teachers as well as the inner experience of reflective dialogue with oneself is paramount. The result is that teachers explore new beginnings and perceive unlimited probabilities; each teacher knows "I can" and "I will."

Freedom to explore, enhanced with security, is ascertainable for teachers, and in Husby's self-directed professional growth program such freedom is shielded yet not outside the political realm of the world. Through the twofold gift of freedom and action in this program, both of which are essential for dynamic learning and professional growth, teachers establish a finer reality of their own; through their own conscious attempts to grow and collaborate, they escape the oppression that belies democracy and learning in schools.

Now is the point at which we decide whether we love and trust teachers and their students enough to share with them the responsibility for their growth. Now is the point at which we refrain from excluding teachers from participation in their own growth and leaving them to their own devices. Now we can and must respond to the opportunity that has opened up for us with the excellence of Husby's new world, one of self-directed and responsible teacher growth previously impossible to conceive of, yet not a mirage. Husby urges us to empower the hidden source of great and beautiful things in education: teachers. Let us begin with the book in your hands.

Preface

Written to seal a proverbial crack in contemporary professional development of educators, this book provides staff developers with the tools, methods, and insight to facilitate individualized teacher learning centered around school and student achievement goals in a group setting. This model is based upon self-directed learning and principles of action research. The primary staff development program can be taken in its entirety and implemented step by step as described, or it can be adapted to meet the unique needs of differing organizations. Overhead costs are very low, as local personnel can facilitate planning and delivery of training sessions.

INTENDED AUDIENCE

The book is written for those who implement professional learning programs for educators: district- and school-level administrators, staff developers, teacher-leaders, instructional coaches, university instructors. Staff development programs derived from this model are meant to be led by a competent, local facilitator as opposed to an outside expert or content-based instructor. Facilitators will gain a foundational understanding of the conceptual ideas behind the program as well as the academic and affective skill sets necessary to lead program activities.

THEORETICAL BACKGROUND

Action research as described by Calhoun (1994) and self-directed learning as advocated by Knowles (1975; Knowles, Holton, & Swanson, 1998; Long & Associates, 1993) were combined to create the infrastructure of the model. Both share several characteristics. They draw on the benefit of addressing learning within a group setting while permitting individual pursuits. Each provides adults an opportunity to pursue learning consistent with their specific needs and interests. Each is problem or life based, an important need for adults. Unlike pure self-directed learning, though, action research inherently provides for evaluation of learning. The benefit of using principles of action research in self-directed learning in staff development, as opposed to utilizing pure action research, is the opportunity for learning in formats other than a research design. By combining action research with self-directed methods, individual needs and preferences of teachers can be met while addressing organizational demands for accountability and improved student achievement.

CONCEPTUAL FRAMEWORK

The framework of the individualized professional development model was drawn from several concepts. Adult learning theory provided the rationale. Self-directed learning dictated the format. Action research presented a method of accountability. Cognitive processing generated by reflection offered a vehicle for deepening participant learning. And a group format created opportunities for professional dialogue and peer support. When implemented in concert, the activities derived from these component pieces work quite well in developing educators' professional knowledge and skill.

ORGANIZATION OF TEXT

Chapter 1 provides the rationale for the model. Chapter 2 lays the foundation for structuring the model's basic professional development program. Chapter 3 explains the guiding structure for individualizing learning—the learning plan. Chapters 4 through 7 delve comprehensively into facilitating the basic professional development program, with a focus on aligning teacher learning with student achievement goals. Chapters 8 and 9 describe procedures for incorporating the self-directed model into a larger school reform program or tailoring it to address organizational needs. Chapter 10 relates typical participant responses, and Chapter 11 reviews a concluding set of "do's and do nots" for program success.

SPECIAL FEATURES

Because the book was designed as a "How To" manual, several instructional components are included:

1. Step-by-step directions for designing and implementing a program, with hints for success

2. Detailed agendas for implementing the basic staff development program

3. Mini-lesson directions and materials

4. Participant examples of learning plans

5. Reproducible learning plan template

6. Reproducible materials for use in a larger reform model professional development program

7. Typical teacher commentary in response to the program

ACKNOWLEDGMENTS

A project that reaches the magnitude of becoming a book is never completely nurtured by a single mind. And this book, in its various incarnations, has grown from the support and pruning of a wide variety of individuals. University professors, administrators, teachers, peer reviewers, friends—all have made critical contributions that led to publication of this work.

Jo Blase encouraged me to pursue doctoral work in educational leadership at the University of Georgia. The first spark of inspiration for this model was born in her class as I sought a way to tie what we know about adult learning and effective staff development to a practical delivery model. Through her guidance, and that of Joseph Blase, I delved deeply into the theoretical background and research base necessary to build the model and study teachers' experiences with it. Lew Allen, Laura Bierema, Karen Watkins, and Sally Zepeda, all of the University of Georgia and members of my doctoral committee, provided invaluable support in developing the model's conceptual components.

After its development, teachers' experiences with the program had to be studied. I am grateful to the teachers and administrators at Richards Middle School for their willingness to participate in the inaugural run of the program. As my supervisors in the roles of university professor, assistant principal, curriculum coordinator, and instructional coach, I am grateful to the following for the free rein allowed me in implementing versions of the model: the University of Georgia Department of Education Leadership, Steve Miletto, Tommy Richardson, Harvey Franklin, Carole Hicks, and Jimmy Stokes. Without their trust and support, there would have been no further development of the model's applications.

The multitude of teachers who participated in various runs of the model offered a highly critical contribution to the professional development programs—feedback and reflections on their experiences, what worked and what did not, and how to improve the program to better serve them. As well, anonymous peer reviewers from across the country, coordinated by Corwin Press, contributed to refinement of the book and its focus on education's ultimate goal: student achievement. Without this broad input, the book would have fallen short in its potential usefulness, application, and effectiveness.

Finally, I would like to thank my friends and family for sharing in this journey with me. Angela Patrick and Lamont Pearson both spent late nights working beside me so I could finish just a little more of each dissertation draft. My "Daddy Too," Col. William J. Quinn, pushed me to "do something different." My parents, my husband's parents, and our friends patiently allowed me time and space to work when they really wanted to visit together. I am grateful for such fantastically supportive loved ones in my life. And last but not least, my husband, Barry Husby, has my undying appreciation. He has quietly convinced me to do more with my talents than I ever thought I could.

The contributions of the following reviewers are gratefully acknowledged:

Dr. Alana L. Mraz
Assistant Superintendent of Educational Service
Lake Forest School District 67
Lake Forest, IL

Susan N. Imamura
Principal
Manoa Elementary School
Honolulu, HI

Dr. Theron J. Schutte
Boone Middle School Principal/Superintendent
Boone Community School District
Boone, IA

Debora Zeis
Teacher
Charlotte Public Schools
Charlotte, MI

Catherine Kilfoyle Duffy
English Language Arts Chairperson
Three Village Central School District
East Setauket, NY

Susan Mundry
Associate Director
Mathematics, Science, and Technology Programs
WestEd
Stoneham, MA

Mike Ford
Superintendent of Schools
Phelps-Clifton Springs Central School District
Clifton Springs, NY

Deborah Childs-Bowen
Assistant Professor
Samford University
Birmingham, AL

Marti Richardson
Past President
National Staff Development Council
Knoxville, TN

Margo M. Marvin
Superintendent of Schools
Putnam Public Schools
Putnam, CT

About the Author

Vicki R. Husby is a curriculum specialist and instructional coach with Walton County Schools in Georgia. She is a former daycare teacher, public school teacher, assistant principal, and assistant professor of "Supervision of Instruction" at the University of Georgia. She received her EdD in educational leadership at the University of Georgia after studying teachers' experiences with self-directed staff development. She holds educational credentials in elementary education, middle grades education, gifted education, special education, and educational leadership. Her areas of expertise include professional development and teacher development, academic interventions, and program development. Her professional experience has been shaped by teaching and leadership roles at middle school, high school, district office, and university levels.

Dr. Husby was selected as the *Atlanta Journal-Constitution's* 2000 Honor Teacher for her work with middle grades at-risk students. She is the editor and a coauthor of the annual *Teacher's Guide for O, Georgia Too: An Awesome Collection of Original Writings by Young Georgians*. Her nonfiction narrative, "Like Mother," was published in *O, Georgia: A Collection of Georgia's Newest and Most Promising Writers, Volume 3*.

Introduction

Meeting Every Teacher's Needs

The No Child Left Behind Act of 2001 put in place a framework for overhauling education in the United States. The driving force behind it was to ensure that schools planned methodically for the education of academically at-risk and advanced students. Use of data was to be key in planning for and assessing improvement, and proven strategies and programs were to be incorporated into schools' plans for improvement. The legislation even mandated that schools analyze data for each student who fails when planning for remediation. Creators of the law left no doubt as to their intent: Individuals' needs must be met to achieve the end of academic success. The intent of this book is to provide a similar framework, albeit much simplified, for ensuring that individual teachers' professional learning needs are met. Such a framework is necessary because, despite definitions of staff development as ongoing individual growth in the context of one's professional role, the typical staff development program for teachers is composed of lectures or demonstrations. Almost never does it incorporate personalized instruction addressing specific teachers' needs (Deojay & Pennington, 2000; National Staff Development Council, 1994). Strangely enough, teachers have clearly stated that when they can direct their professional growth activities, learning is meaningful and results in knowledge and skill improvement (Corabi, 1995; Husby, 2002). The difficulty in meeting teachers' individual needs thus far has been the availability of programs focused upon such an end.

A FORMAT FOR INDIVIDUALIZING LEARNING

Self-directed learning is simply what it sounds like: direction of a person's learning by himself or herself. When this occurs, learning cannot be any more individualized, since the individual makes every choice about what is learned, how it is learned, and what constitutes success. Adults informally learn in this format all the time, with large to small projects, across brief to more extensive spans of time (Long & Associates, 1993).

The professional growth model described in this book is built around an individualized, self-directed format for learning. The specific staff development program growing from the model is designed to be delivered to a group by a facilitator. It incorporates only four activities during group meetings: completion of a learning plan, mini-lessons to develop self-directedness, independent work on a self-selected project, and individual and group reflections. In order to preserve the purpose of the model—individualized development—at least two-thirds of each session is devoted to independent work.

PARTS OF THE PROGRAM

The goal of self-directed professional development is to lead educators to identify areas for professional improvement, and then to assist them in guiding their own development in a particular growth area. The program rests upon the following four components, which will be discussed in depth:

- **Learning Plan.** The learning plan guides planning for goal focus and methods of gathering and responding to information, transferring learning to practice, and assessing goal achievement.
- **Mini-Lessons.** Mini-lessons focus on skills and information that aid learners in developing self-directedness. Specifically, lessons center on gathering and interpreting various forms of information and data.
- **Learning Project.** Participants may work individually or with a group to complete a project of their choice. Project selection is based upon a combination of self-identified growth areas, professional responsibilities, school and district goals, and a direct connection to student achievement.
- **Reflections.** Each session begins with updates on progress and a statement of the plan for independent work time. Each session closes with a written reflection of the learners' choice on any aspect of the program or their learning.

These activities are led by a facilitator knowledgeable in adult learning or with prior experience and training in such a program.

HOW LEARNERS RESPOND

For first-time participants in this form of professional development, the range of responses is interesting to say the very least. Typically, the learners expect, contrary to the claim that their learning is to be self-directed, that the facilitator will *tell* them exactly what to do and how to do it. After a couple of weeks, the realization sets in that they are truly in control of their learning. At this point, an array of emotions is experienced, from anger as individuals hit barriers to pure elation when they make leaps toward completing their projects. At the conclusion of the program, the vast number of learners are pleased with their handiwork and subsequently the opportunity to have their specific needs met. The single complaint about the program is that it takes time away from something else, but the realization that this is the case with any staff development is offered as an off-setting point by participants.

HOW THIS IS DIFFERENT FROM TRADITIONAL STAFF DEVELOPMENT

Districts and schools have historically relied upon external expertise to provide development activities for their educators, and staff development has consisted of one-day workshops designed around a district goal. Rarely is the information implemented in classrooms (Black, 1998; Collinson, 2000). Participants are generally passive recipients as opposed to collaborative designers of professional learning.

Conversely, in learning organizations, individual schools and their faculties are central in determining needs and planning professional growth activities (Georgia Department of Education, 1997). As the Georgia Department of Education noted, school-focused professional development becomes a process as opposed to an event. As a result, collective learning shifts the model of learning from one-day workshops to learning that is embedded in teachers' roles (Collinson, 2000). As a function of developing the knowledge and skills of personnel to achieve school development, school-focused professional development programs are designed to incorporate adult learning theory and address individual learning needs of educators (Georgia Department of Education, 1997). Zeichner, Klehr, and Caro-Bruce (2000) contended,

> Good professional development respects and builds upon the knowledge and expertise that teachers already have. It allows participants to control and drive the opportunity, and involves inquiry and reflection over time with colleagues about issues that matter most to the teachers involved. (p. 36)

To be clear, the vast difference between this self-directed model and traditional staff development is how content is determined, delivered, and assessed. It is the difference between a learning-focused and a sit-and-get model.

In planning for learning through the self-directed model, participants brainstorm interest and growth areas with accompanying background data, then list their job responsibilities. Job responsibilities incorporate school and district goals drawn from student achievement data. From the two lists, a single topic for focus is identified by each participant. Individuals are then led to methodically develop a comprehensive plan for study in the focus area, again considering the impact of their learning on student achievement. Inherent to the plan is a method for assessing knowledge and skill, both at the onset and conclusion of the program, as well as the effects of learning and its application to student achievement. Learning is guided, not delivered, by a facilitator knowledgeable in adult learning. It occurs over time as a process and is job-embedded—directly connected to participants' roles.

Succinctly stated, the primary differences between this model and those historically used are the individualization of learning, development of participants in self-direction of professional learning, and use of a facilitator rather than "an instructor." And in terms of results, all participants have reported either use or intended use of knowledge and skill gained in their professional roles. As well, they noted a direct meeting of their individual needs—in both content and learning style.

ADDRESSING NSDC'S STANDARDS FOR STAFF DEVELOPMENT

Black (1998) found that schools achieving results through staff development implemented programs that aligned with the school's long-term goals for school improvement and student achievement, were derived from research, and adhered to the National Staff Development Council's (NSDC) Standards for Staff Development. The NSDC's 12 standards established an expected level of performance for staff development and are "grounded in research that documents the connection between staff development and student learning" (NSDC, 2001, p. 2). They are organized into three categories: context, process, and content.

Table 1.1 illustrates how the standards and their accompanying expectations are addressed within the self-directed professional development program.

The staff development program was designed to incorporate what was known about adult learning principles, provide for accountability, and adhere to effective staff development practices. For this reason, it naturally aligns with the NSDC's standards and expectations.

CONCEPTUAL FRAMEWORK

In order to provide a more complete understanding of the individualized professional development program for facilitators, each of the concepts

Table 1.1   Relationship Between NSDC Standards and Program Components

Standard	Expectation	Program Component
Context	Adults are organized into learning communities, and their goals align with school and district goals.	• Delivered in a group setting • Group and individual reflection • Individual goals connected to school and district goals
	School and district leaders will be skillful in guiding continuous school improvement.	• School or district level facilitator guides sessions and ensures participants are aligned with school and district goals.
	Resources are provided to support learning and collaboration among adults.	• Training takes place in a location where computers and online resources are available and adults can work together in small groups.
Process	Staff development programs are data driven.	• School and district goals are based upon needs assessments. Individuals' goals must align with school and district goals and connect directly to student achievement.
	Evaluation is incorporated.	• Participants must assess their knowledge/skill level at the onset and conclusion of the program and demonstrate growth. • Student achievement data may be used to demonstrate improvement in teachers' knowledge and skill. • The impact of learning on student achievement must be accounted for in planning and assessed when the program concludes.
	Staff development programs are research based.	• Self-directed learning and action research, the framework of the program, have been proven effective in impacting student achievement.
	Staff development programs are designed according to intended goals.	• Participants determine their focus area and goal at the onset of the program. All activities are designed toward goal attainment.
	Knowledge about learning is applied in delivering training.	• Adult learning principles, reflection, and professional learning groups are central to the program design.
	Educators' ability to collaborate is developed.	• Small group activities, group reflection, and the option to work with others on a project address collaboration.

(Continued)

Table 1.1 (Continued)

Standard	Expectation	Program Component
Content	Equity is addressed by developing understanding and appreciation for all students, impacting the learning environment created, and generating expectations for academic achievement.	• A format for individualized learning within a group context is modeled. • Focus area and goal must impact student achievement.
	Quality teaching is supported through deepening of educators' knowledge of content, strategies, and assessment.	• Individuals' goals must impact student achievement, and therefore content, strategies, and assessment are naturally addressed.
	Family involvement is encouraged by training educators to solicit and engage families in student learning.	*This expectation is not inherently addressed in the program.*

supporting the model will be briefly explained. While the explanations provide only a cursory review of each topic, they should be sufficient to clarify how the pieces of the program work together.

Adult Learning Theory

According to Eduard Lindeman, a pioneer in adult learning theory, "every adult person finds himself in specific situations . . . which call for adjustments. Adult education begins and ends at this point" (Lindeman, 1926, p. 6). Lindeman was of the opinion that subject matter should be brought to the situation and the curriculum built around adult learners' needs and interests. He held five key assumptions about adult learners (Knowles et al., 1998):

- Adults are motivated to learn as their needs and interests require it
- Their orientation to learning is life centered
- Experience is their most valuable resource
- Adults have an inherent need to self-direct their learning
- As individuals age, the differences between them increase

Lindeman asserted, "Authoritative teaching, examinations which preclude original thinking, rigid pedagogical formula—all of these have no place in adult education" (Lindeman, 1926, p. 7).

Lindeman (1926) contended that adults want their talents to be used, to express themselves to others, and foremost, to improve themselves. He stated the spirit and meaning of adult education is not found in formalized educational settings, but in small groups of adults who learn through confronting pertinent situations, who reach into the reservoirs of their experience before reaching for a textbook, and who are led in discussion by teachers who are co-learners.

Malcolm Knowles, known as the father of contemporary adult learning theory (Knowles et al., 1998), also noted that each adult learner's needs and situation differ, and therefore adults are best served when learning is adapted to their "uniqueness" and situational needs. He related six key assumptions that differentiated adult learning from that of children's learning (Knowles et al., 1998):

- Adult learners have a need to know the "what, how and why" of learning
- Their self-concept must be that of an autonomous, self-directing learner
- Prior experience must be used as a resource and understood to contribute to the learner's "mental mode"
- Readiness to learn is life related and based upon developmental tasks
- Adult learners' orientation to learning is problem centered and contextual
- Motivation to learn is intrinsic and incorporates a personal benefit

Knowles stated that the adult "comes into an educational activity largely because he is experiencing some inadequacy in coping with current life problems. He wants to apply tomorrow what he learns today" (Knowles, 1975, p. 48). Knowles proposed self-directed learning as the way to meet specific needs of adult learners.

Self-Directed Learning

Self-directed learning is based on the idea of learner control, as opposed to the role of instructors as sole decision makers. Garrison (1993) listed three factors that had to be present in order for individuals to be in control of their learning: independence to choose goals, support in the form of human and nonhuman resources to achieve goals, and personal ability required to achieve goals. Self-directed learning often will incorporate shared control, combining learner input and the legitimate role of the teacher.

Tough, who studied adults' learning projects and held a slightly different view of adult learning than Knowles, stated that adults' chief motivation for learning is goal-oriented (Bonham, 1992). He noted learning at their own pace, in their own style, in flexible ways, and in their own structure as reasons adults chose to learn on their own (Tough, 1992). Tough discussed two goal types: extrinsic and intrinsic (Olgren, 1993). With an extrinsic goal, learning is directed to an end outside the person, such as a reward or promotion. In meeting this type of goal, the learner primarily seeks to reproduce facts, and use of learning is minimal. Intrinsic goals come from within the person and involve use of learning for personal reasons, such as self-improvement. Learners motivated by intrinsic goals become more deeply and personally engaged in learning experiences. Tough (1992) stated that in relation to work, learners do not engage in learning because they cannot perform the job, but instead they learn because they want to do a *good* job.

Tough listed four major benefits of self-directed learning for adults (Kasworm, 1992): It is specific to the learner's needs and preferences; learning is under the individual's control; learning opportunities are available even when expert courses or materials are not; and lastly, it is convenient for the learner.

While Tough focused on self-directed learning by adults working independently, Knowles chose to concentrate his work on self-directed learning within a group setting. Knowles described four characteristics of self-directed learning in a group:

- Adult learners become more self-directed over time
- Responsibility for learning is placed on individual learners
- A climate of warmth, respect, support, and trust is emphasized
- The learner may need assistance in becoming a proficient self-directed learner (Long & Associates, 1993)

Knowles strongly suggested respect be given to adult learners and the experiences they bring, while simultaneously nurturing them to develop their self-directedness.

Although Knowles was a prominent advocate for self-directed learning, he recognized there are situations when teacher-led instruction may be preferred (Knowles, 1989). One such situation is when the learner has little or no experience with the topic being explored. Another is when the learner is under external pressure to master a large amount of subject matter. Even in these cases, Knowles noted the importance of critical thinking on the part of learners to ensure growth.

Action Research

Action research is the investigation, by educators, into the effectiveness of instructional practices and programs within their schools (Calhoun, 1994). The process includes five basic phases: (a) identification of an interest area or problem, (b) collection of baseline data, (c) organization of data, (d) interpretation of data as related to the interest area or problem, and (e) implementation of an action plan in response to data. This framework for improvement is cyclical; based on data and outcomes, subsequent interest or problem areas are identified, then the process repeats. Whether conducted by individual teachers or groups of colleagues, Calhoun (1994) found the benefit of action research to be the potential for individuals to develop a professional mindset and improve their performance by becoming adept problem solvers.

Action research has been employed in a variety of formats (Auger & Wideman, 2000; Feldman, 1998; Poetter, McKamey, Ritter, & Tisdel, 1999; Robertson, 2000; Sardo-Brown, 1995; Vulliamy, 1991). While the particular approaches to action research vary, the basic methods, benefits, and constraints of the process are fairly common. Often research is conducted by those working in a school. Conversation with facilitators and peers is highly beneficial in advancing learning. Overwhelmingly, participants express intent to apply the knowledge gained in their professional roles. And of particular importance, reflection is repeatedly described as the key to creating change, and successful action researchers have noted the provision of time to reflect during the process.

Reflection

Mezirow (2000) stated that individuals' identity and reality are shaped by their cultures and relationships. According to his theory of transformational learning, one must confront ingrained beliefs and critically reflect upon them in order to transform and grow. He asserts the vehicle for reflection is collaborative discussion with others, where different perspectives are presented and viewpoints challenging norms are encouraged. True growth, or transformational learning, occurs in four ways according to Mezirow: by stating current thoughts, by learning new thoughts, by transforming thoughts, or by changing mental habits. He contended that aiding adults to become autonomous thinkers is both a method and a goal for adult educators.

Professional Learning Groups

Through group learning, staff developers can offer adults opportunities for intellectual challenge and stimulation within a safe setting (Murphy, 1999; Zeichner et al., 2000). Murphy found that teacher study groups can impact not only students, but also the school's overall culture, assumptions, beliefs, and behaviors. Tichenor and Heins (2000) found that faculty members of schools using study groups reported the groups made a significant contribution to achievement of school goals. Hirsch and Sparks (1999) noted that learning teams that are successful solve common problems, meet weekly and set incremental goals, analyze results after implementation, and discuss instructional methods. Tichenor and Heins added that successful group learning occurs when participation is voluntary, activities encourage participation, time is provided for implementation and reflection, and participants are included in selection of materials.

Tichenor and Heins (2000) stated, "The process of exploring questions and sharing solutions in a trusting and supportive environment paves the way for renewed teaching and learning and facilitates the development of professional learning communities" (p. 317). They offer the following guidelines for success when organizing collaborative groups: Permit voluntary participation, allow participants to determine topics and activities for study in relation to school goals, permit time for implementation and reflection, provide incentives for remaining in the group, include a reasonable number of members, and provide assistance to the group in getting started. Murphy (1999) suggested that within a group, all members should have equal status so that no participant is deferred to because of title, degree level, or other factors of rank. As well, Murphy contended, equal status encourages more productive group participation, as the underlying assumption is that all members have something of value to contribute to the group. In essence, collaborative group learning is built upon understanding and respect for each group member's perspectives and the development of skills for effectively communicating and addressing group goals.

CONCLUSION

The framework of the self-directed professional development program was designed to account for the developmental and professional needs of educators while responding to larger school goals. The purpose of this book is to provide a model for individualizing professional learning. As a whole, the model provides an inexpensive, versatile, personalized approach to simultaneously addressing teacher needs, organizational goals, and student achievement.

The model includes four components: completion of a learning plan, mini-lessons to develop self-directedness, independent work on a self-selected project, and individual and group reflections. Across the professional development program, participants often experience a range of emotions as they encounter barriers and find successes. This model is founded upon self-directed learning and incorporates the guidance of a facilitator as opposed to an instructor. It is fundamentally different from traditional staff development in that each participant has control over his or her development, and learning occurs through a job-embedded program. The model is designed around what is known about adult learning and effective staff development, and it closely aligns with the National Staff Development Council's Standards for Staff Development. The conceptual framework draws upon adult learning theory, self-directed learning, action research, reflection, and professional learning groups.

2

Structuring the Professional Development Program

The structure of the individualized staff development program greatly impacts the degree of success participants can achieve, but it can be effectively organized in a number of different formats. The bulk of this book (Chapters 2 through 7) will describe in detail the basic format found by the author to be most successful. Later chapters will address incorporation of the program into a larger reform model (Chapter 8) and adjusting the format to meet your organization's needs (Chapter 9), including models requiring less facilitator support. Chapter 11 will provide several do's and do nots to consider as you structure your own program. As long as the major components of the program are maintained, you should feel free to experiment with the structure until you find one that best suits you.

Factors to Consider in Planning

When, How Often, and Where to Meet

Materials and Their Organization

Selecting an Appropriate Facilitator

Philosophy:
This is a venture to empower adults to develop themselves.

DETERMINING WHEN, HOW OFTEN, AND WHERE TO MEET

For most educators, time is precious, and scheduling sessions when they cannot settle into solid mental activity sets the stage for very frustrated participants. And, since the whole program works upon individuals' developing themselves, lack of quality opportunities to do so sets up both the people and the program to fail. Therefore, much care and thought should be put into determining when and where to meet so as to preserve the benefits of the learning format.

Determining When to Meet

For job-embedded learning, or learning taking place within the context of a person's role, finding time for deep thought presents a problem. Most educators, regardless of their specific roles, will tell you time for heavy-duty contemplation is almost nonexistent during the traditional workday. It is because of this, and the desire to maintain a connection between learning and its application in the classroom, that the initial staff development sessions were held just after the school day ended.

The individualized staff development framework was based upon Knowles's (1975) eight-session self-directed group model that incorporated the following schedule:

- Session 1: orientation, setting the climate, building relationships
- Session 2: determining needs and objectives for learning
- Session 3: creating a learning plan
- Session 4: revising/adjusting learning plans; working with teams
- Sessions 5 through 7: working with teams
- Sessions 8: presentations on learning

It naturally flowed that eight sessions would drive planning of the program. In the inaugural run of the program, the number of sessions worked out well, providing ample time for individuals to complete their learning projects without providing much time for goofing off. In a later run of the program, 13 shorter sessions were held during school planning periods, but opportunities for the participants to engage mentally in their own tasks were reduced, as group and individual reflections took the same amount of daily time as in the eight longer sessions. As well, teachers were not able to devote the full planning period to learning tasks due to myriad other demands upon them during the workday. It was easier for folks in the eight-session afterschool groups to stay focused on their tasks for the duration of each session and the program. And, I found my role as facilitator less taxing when we worked with a more lengthy session.

Determining How Often to Meet

In planning the number and length of sessions, it is important to remember the activities that have to be accomplished. During each session, time should be provided for development of self-directed skills, planning, group reflection, individual reflection, and independent work. Skill development, planning, and reflection take time, since individuals are mentally processing their experiences and what they have learned. And, since the goal of the program is to have participants complete a learning project, ample time must be provided to work on the project. While participants should feel free to work on their projects outside of the sessions, it should be *clearly communicated* that outside work is not required as part of the program.

The length of the staff development sessions was originally guided by state requirements for earning staff development units (SDUs) toward certificate renewal. The mandate required 10 seat hours for one SDU. That meant the participant had to be present with the program instructor for each hour counted toward an SDU. Since it had already been determined the original group would meet for eight sessions, and that there would be individual and group reflections, mini-lessons, and independent work, sessions had to be long enough to accommodate activities without fatiguing people who had already put in a full day's work. It was clear 10 hours would be insufficient to develop the learners' self-directed skills *and* provide them time to complete a learning project. It neatly worked out that 8 sessions of 2.5 hours equaled 20 seat hours, the equivalent of 2 SDUs. In planning your own program, consider state requirements for earning SDUs. It is easy enough to lengthen individual work time to account for additional staff development hours.

After determining the number of seat hours the program would comprise, each session was planned with the following agenda in mind: 15 minutes for verbal group reflection on progress and commitment to the day's work plan, 30 minutes or less for a mini-lesson, 90 minutes of individual work time, and 15 minutes for closing and individual written reflections (see Table 2.1). In your own program, if opening group sharing runs beyond 15 minutes, time spent on the mini-lesson should be reduced. The priority activity of each session is independent work time. For those who choose to write the individual reflection as they process their learning, the final 15 minutes is simply extended work time.

When planning each session, a good rule of thumb is that 60%–65% of each session should be devoted to independent work time. Individuals will need time to organize their belongings and become immersed in the work. A minimum of an hour should be given for this activity, but an hour and a half is even better.

Work on both the learning plan and mini-lessons addresses development of self-directed skills, and these activities occur during the 30 minutes set aside for the mini-lesson. It is not necessary to use all 30 minutes; any remaining time can be given for independent work. It is important,

Table 2.1   Structure of Sessions

Session	First 15 Minutes	Next 30 Minutes	Body of Session 90 Minutes	Final 15 Minutes
1	Introductions, Climate Setting	Orientation to Model	Brainstorm Interest/Growth Areas, Define Responsibilities	Individual Reflection
2	Group Reflection	*Learning Plan*: Identifying Focus, Defining the Problem, Planning for Self-Directed Study, Self-Directed Study (Research/ Data Gathering Section) *Mini-Lesson:* Introduce Template for Evaluating Written Material	Individual Work Time	Individual Reflection
3	Group Reflection	*Learning Plan*: Self-Directed Study (Pre-Project Assessment, Summary/ Interpretation of Pre-Project Assessment Sections) *Mini-Lesson:* Critically Evaluating Information Using Template from Sessio 2, Demonstrate How to Use Online Databases to Gather Information	Individual Work Time	Individual Reflection
4	Group Reflection	*Mini-Lesson:* Basic Terminology of Qualitative and Quantitative Research	Individual Work Time	Individual Reflection
5	Group Reflection	*Learning Plan:* Self-Directed Learning (Interpretation of Research/Data Gathering, Translating New Knowledge/Skills into Plan to Meet Goals Sections)	Individual Work Time	Individual Reflection
6	Group Reflection	*Mini-Lesson:* Gathering Alternate Forms of Data in Your Classroom/Role	Individual Work Time	Individual Reflection
7	Group Reflection	*Learning Plan:* Self-Directed Learning (Implementation of Plan to Meet Goals Section)	Individual Work Time	Individual Reflection
8	Group Reflection	*Learning Plan:* Self-Directed Learning (Post-Project Assessment, ummary/Interpretation of Post-Project Assessment Sections)	Presentations	Individual Reflection

though, not to spend more than the allotted time on these activities, as participants are easily fatigued at the end of a workday. As well, they often want to move on to "their" part of the session—individual work time.

Determining Where to Meet

To be effective, the staff development sessions must be conducted in an environment that does not limit or impair potential for learning. The runs of the program that were most successful took place in school media centers that had computers, printers, and ample workspace in the form of tables. Participants had the flexibility to gather information via the Internet, work on data organization, prepare items for their projects, and interact with personal materials without having to leave or cart around belongings. As well, the facilitator was able to ensure that all participants were spending the session time on staff development activities and not other items.

In one run of the program, when the staff development sessions were conducted during the school day, the media center was being used by classroom teachers and students. The environment was not amenable to deep thought, nor was it free from disruption. While it was easy enough to find a large office space or classroom, the availability of computer resources for all participants was greatly reduced. Also, while there was ample space between adult bodies, there was not necessarily ample space for spreading out a number of resources on top of student desks. In another run, even when graduate students in adult-sized desks tried to work in a university classroom, there did not seem to be enough room to spread out and work efficiently. The sum total of the experiences was lack of learner engagement, and as a facilitator, I felt guilty for requiring these adults to sit there and ultimately have to do the work on their own time.

When participants are forced to leave the location to have the tools, space, and quiet they need, time for work and accountability for on-task activity drastically declines, and effectiveness of the model for the group as a whole diminishes. The "greater good" of on-task activity is that learners are progressing and growing. To be certain, adults have deep needs to be respected and in control of their world. If the facilitator is perceived to be undermining either of these needs by acting as a guardian rather than a peer, learners will withdraw the only thing they have to give—genuine cooperation. Consequently, facilitators should consider in advance the actions they will take to ensure on-task behavior. Facilitators must find a way to subtly supervise without coming off as "Big Brother." I found circulating within the group, offering assistance, and asking questions like "How are you pulling things together today?" provided subtle prompts for on-task work.

MATERIALS AND THEIR ORGANIZATION

In conducting various runs of the staff development program, the same basic materials were utilized: learning plan, mini-lesson materials, and journal pages. What varied from run to run was the use of a published agenda and how the materials were organized and presented to the participants. A simple trend permeated all the runs—the more organized and detailed the agenda and presentation of materials, the more likely the participants were to remain focused and accountable for both their time and materials.

During the inaugural run of the program, each person was given a crisp, white notebook with tabbed sections. There was a section for the agenda (see Resource A) in which detailed activities for all eight sessions were listed. It described the sequence of activities and gave advance notice of what participants should be prepared to do the next time. There was a tab for the learning plan (see Resource B), and it never had to leave the notebook. The remaining sections were for individual meeting days, and each had a copy of the session's agenda, all the materials for the mini-lesson, and a journal page. During this run, no one lost materials, not a single person had to hunt for mini-lesson resources, and sessions ran like clockwork.

In later runs, due to cost of materials and experimentation in structure and agenda, participants were given a folder with pockets. In the left pocket was a copy of the learning plan. In the right pocket was a complete set of the mini-lesson materials and journal pages. As the facilitator, only I had a copy of the agenda, and I shared it aloud at the beginning of each session. Individuals participating in these runs, especially those meeting during the school day, seemed more disorganized as a group. Mini-lesson resources were harder for them to find, individuals could not easily locate the next journal page, and the group as a whole seemed to regularly confuse mini-lesson materials with the learning plan. This same disorganization flowed over into management of their personal materials for the learning projects.

Even though the same activities occurred in all runs, and those without the agenda were told what would be occurring for the session, the group that had their own copy of the agenda seemed to capitalize upon the visual reminder. They clicked through session activities more efficiently and did not rely solely upon the facilitator to jumpstart each transition. They knew from the agenda what was occurring, and they aided in keeping the session on track. As well, they consistently came with their personal materials and had no difficulty distinguishing between the plan and mini-lesson activities. Overall, the more organized and efficient the materials are, the more organized and efficient the participants are. The facilitator, I found, inadvertently sets the standard.

SELECTING AN APPROPRIATE FACILITATOR

Blase and Blase (1998) found that good instructional leaders, as defined by teachers, conversed often and openly with teachers about instruction, provided time for collaboration among teachers, empowered teachers by allowing autonomy in decision making, and understood and confronted change and its challenges. Additionally, Acheson and Gall (1997) found that teachers desire an instructional leader meet with them individually, engage in conversation regarding their concerns, provide assistance in collecting and analyzing data, demonstrate skill in teaching and supervision, and provide support. Further, Acheson and Gall noted that in leading a group of teachers, an effective instructional supervisor communicated expectations clearly, was enthusiastic, employed a variety of strategies and activities, and kept the group on task. In essence, an effective instructional leader demonstrates knowledge of school concerns as well as teacher needs and provides for individual and group processes to address to both (Guskey, 1995).

For this staff development program to work, it is critical that the right facilitator be chosen. It must be someone who

- Theoretically and practically understands adult learning
- Has a command of instructional practices
- Can freely allow participants to make their own learning choices
- Can succinctly present a mini-lesson
- Can support learners during displays of emotion
- Can keep a group on track
- Understands the role to be that of facilitator and not content instructor
- Has had experience with self-directed learning

This individual must be willing to repeatedly remind participants that they make all the decisions about the project. Patience is essential in empowering the group to take control of their own learning because all initially think there is a catch somewhere, and they *will* be told *exactly* what to do. As one teacher stated,

> We've always been in these classes, even in poetry where there is no right or wrong answer. You break down a piece of poetry into what it means to you, but I was still told I was wrong. Well, they told me there's no right or wrong, but then they told me what I did wasn't good enough . . . You just never truly believe there is no right or wrong.

A working understanding of adult learning packs a big bang in the making of a successful facilitator. In Chapter 1, a brief description of adult learning theory was presented. For a more thorough treatment of the topic, I highly recommend *The Adult Learner: The Definitive Classic in Adult Education and Human Resources Development* (5th ed.) by Knowles, Holton, and Swanson (1998). The authors provide excellent coverage of history, theory, and application.

While it is not necessary that the facilitator go through training for this professional development program, as the book provides a clear explanation, it is strongly suggested the person experience this type of learning before attempting to lead a group. Experience can be gained by fully conducting a project using the learning plan, in advance of facilitating a professional learning program. It is much easier to be understanding and supportive when you have some idea of what learners are experiencing. Those who have gone through the agony of planning, conducting, and defending research for a dissertation have had a very similar experience.

The parallel is that in writing a dissertation, the learner has had to set a specific goal, collect all the background data and resources, use that information for some other purpose, determine when the goal is met, and then present the work to others for approval. The catch is that in writing a dissertation, learners set a standard of quality for themselves, and because these individuals know what they are capable of doing, the goal set is usually much more challenging than a goal someone else would set for them. Subsequently, all the frustration, angst, intermittent insecurity, and desire to meet that goal must be ploughed through as a natural part of trying to achieve the goal. In this program, while only the learner determines goal completion, he always knows in the back of his mind his peers will be viewing the final product, and the need to appear in a positive light is ever present.

Academic Knowledge and Skills Needed by the Facilitator

Basic Knowledge of Qualitative and Quantitative Data

Basic Knowledge of Data Collection, Organization, and Analysis

Proficiency in Locating Professional Resources Through Both Traditional and Online Methods

Clear Understanding of and Commitment to the Philosophy Behind Self-Directed Learning

---

The facilitator will be key in leading participants to success. This person will have to provide assurance that is it alright for learners to pursue their own goals, in their own way, and in the manner they learn best. School counselors can provide assistance with reading verbal and nonverbal cues and responding in a manner to encourage discourse. The facilitator will also have to be familiar with data gathering, organization, and analysis in order to deliver mini-lessons and assist participants with these activities. District-level testing and research personnel are usually a good resource for learning these skills. As well, the facilitator must be adept at finding various types of information and resources so that guidance can be given to others in their learning pursuits. Modern media specialists, instructional technology specialists, and local town or university librarians can often provide assistance with these skills. And finally, the facilitator must live the philosophy behind this model: The purpose of self-directed professional development is to empower educators to develop themselves professionally.

PHILOSOPHY

The philosophy behind the model is that this is a venture to empower adults to develop themselves. Every decision that is made about the structure of the program will impact the degree to which this philosophy is maintained. Without a sufficient number of sessions, and without time and space for support and independent work in those sessions, the mental processes necessary for growth cannot take place. Without clear organization of sessions and materials, learners will not come to clearly understand the process and what they are to do. A competent facilitator is the key to a successful experience for the teachers, school, and district.

The philosophy behind the program provides a critical reminder of its purpose. We are addressing student achievement and organizational goals by way of creating a cadre of self-directed educators. We are empowering teachers and leaders to continually develop themselves professionally.

CONCLUSION

A good deal of front-end time should be spent carefully organizing the when, how often, where, and materials of the staff development program. As well, a facilitator should be selected based upon the qualities necessary to guide others in successful self-directed learning. Remember, the better prepared the program, materials, and facilitator are in advance, the more likely it is that participants will mirror the same. Finally, the philosophy behind the model provides a critical reminder of its purpose: This is a venture to empower adults to develop themselves professionally.

3

The Learning Plan

The learning plan is a tool to guide participants through the mental steps of methodically planning for and responding to learning. It is a comprehensive document that is meant to be completed across the course of the program. By completing it in phases, participants are led in critical learning processes: drawing on experiences, evaluating actions, and reflecting on learning. The learning plan is the cornerstone of the individualized, self-directed model, and it constructs the foundation for the learning project.

Without the learning plan, the most beneficial facets of this model are lost. Besides learning processes, accountability for learning is also removed in the absence of the plan. In essence, without the learning plan, the project is simply an activity—an activity that is without the inherent developmental properties built into the model. To be certain, the learning plan is essential to well-rounded, individualized professional growth.

LEARNING PROJECTS

Learning projects were defined by Tough (Kasworm, 1992) according to six characteristics. They are created by a question or goal. Understanding is often private and evolving. The project is dynamic in that it may involve many changes in direction. Learning usually occurs in episodes and is focused for a period of time. The learner creates, conducts, and evaluates the learning.

Learning projects conducted through this staff development program are developed within principles of action research. That framework includes five basic phases described by Calhoun (1994): (a) identification of an interest area or problem, (b) collection of baseline data, (c) organization of data, (d) interpretation of data as related to interest area or problem, and (e) implementation of an action plan in response to data. While participants are not expected to conduct research, this format serves as a planner to aid adults in designing, carrying out, and evaluating the learning project. Participants are provided with a written copy of the planner, which I call the learning plan.

The guiding structure of the learning plan has four broad phases:

1. Identifying the focus

2. Defining the problem

3. Planning for self-directed study

4. Self-directed study

Movement through these phases is directed by a series of prompts and questions to which learners respond in writing. When identifying the focus, emphasis is placed on selecting an interest or concern that is directly related to the individual's responsibilities and school and district goals drawn from student achievement data. In defining the problem, desired goals and their link to student achievement, pre- and post-project assessments, and indicators of achievement are described. Planning for self-directed study includes identifying a mode for study, an organizational method, and the time frame for completing the project.

Self-directed study involves implementation of the learning project and its requisite parts: pre-assessment, data gathering, translating knowledge and skills into an action plan, implementation of the action plan, post-assessment, interpretation of results, and a statement of impact of development on the focus area—particularly on student achievement as measured with data. Participants retain the flexibility to adjust components of their plans and projects. Knowledge and skill evolve and change as learning does, and as such, a learning project can be expected to evolve and change in response.

PROGRAM CYCLE AND STAGES

Through direct instruction (Knowles, 1975), whole group discussion (Auger & Wideman, 2000; Feldman, 1998; Knowles, 1975), individual reflection (Auger & Wideman, 2000; Feldman, 1998), and written prompts (Knowles, 1975) on the learning plan, participants are guided through the stages listed in Table 3.1 (Calhoun, 1994).

Table 3.1 is a guide for working through the plan and project in eight weeks. Some participants may finish some stages ahead of or behind schedule. More important than when each person completes each stage is that each completes the project by the final session. What is "complete" is determined by the participant. Again, this may have changed since the onset of the program. Goals may be expanded or minimized in response to the learner's development during the program.

Table 3.1   Stages of the Learning Project

Session	Cycle and Stage
1	Identify interest/growth areas and professional responsibilities
2	Identify focus Define the problem Plan for self-directed study Self-directed study *(determine research/data gathering strategies)*
3	Self-directed study *(pre-project assessment, summary/interpretation of pre-project assessment)*
4	Self-directed study Independent work on research/data gathering
5	Self-directed study *(interpretation of research/data gathering translating new knowledge into a plan to meet goals)*
6	Self-directed study *(translating new knowledge into a plan to meet goals)*
7	Self-directed study *(implementation of plan to meet goals)*
8	Self-directed study *(post-project assessment, summary/interpretation of post-project assessment)* Projects presented to the group

Each stage of the program cycle is composed of specific concepts and activities. Chapters 4 through 7 present a detailed description of the activities corresponding to each stage, in the order the stages occur during the program. Activities are related to their stages in the following order: identifying responsibilities, identifying focus, defining the problem, planning for self-directed study, and self-directed study. Two examples from previous participants' learning plans follow each description. The first example is "Participant A" and traces a single participant's learning plan across the staff development program. The second example is "Another Participant" and includes snapshots of learning plans of teachers across different content areas and grades to demonstrate how the plan was applied in differing roles and situations.

Each of Chapters 4 through 7 provides an introduction to a stage. The chapter is organized according to staff development sessions. The activities of each stage are presented according to the session in which they generally occur. The mini-lessons that accompany that stage and session are described also.

ADAPTING THE PLAN TO MEET YOUR NEEDS

The basic learning plan is provided as Resource B. This generic plan could be used as is within a larger reform model or alternate program structure, with specific directions to participants for setting goals that correspond to their organization's particular purposes. The responsibility of communicating a specific range of goal options would rest with the facilitator.

Another way to specifically target your organization's goals is to modify the learning plan. Primarily, changes to the plan would be made on the first page, where duties and responsibilities are listed. Very simply, prompts specific to responsibilities stemming from your reform model or school initiatives would replace or be added to the plan's general prompts. These slight changes would frame the direction your organization wants to take and leave the self-directed process intact.

Further attention to and examples of modifying the plan will be given in Chapter 8. While this chapter focuses on adapting the plan for a reform model, the same basic changes to the plan would apply when adapting the plan for a school initiative, such as increasing instruction of test-taking strategies.

CONCLUSION

The purpose of the learning plan is to structure thought and planning throughout the staff development program. By completing it incrementally over several weeks, participants are continually focused on the goals they set for themselves. As well, the prompts lead to deeper thought about the purposes and actions behind each goal. The plan itself provides the primary direction needed for participants to methodically develop themselves and self-direct their learning. It may be implemented as is or adapted to focus on initiatives specific to a particular organization.

Some critics may comment that the plan itself is rather lengthy. It is important to remember, though, that the program is not just about completing a project. If that were the case, a learning plan would not be necessary. The larger purpose of the plan and program components is to guide educators in developing self-directedness in professional learning. Growth can come only from continual, ongoing learning in a job-embedded context. Through both planning and reflective prompts, systematic thinking about the focus area is guided across time, lending opportunity for real professional growth.

4

Working From the Learning Plan

Identifying Focus

The first two sessions of the staff development program lead participants toward identifying a focus for self-directed study. Sometimes individuals come to the program knowing what they would like to pursue, and this stage of the process is quite easy. Other participants, while knowing from the program description that they will pursue an independent project, still think the facilitator will tell them what to do. In either case, each learner is asked to go through the initial planning stages so that certain necessities can be met.

Of particular importance in the early planning stages is that each person selects a focus area and goal that meet the following three criteria:

- Relates to professional responsibilities
- Aligns with school and district goals
- Impacts student achievement in a manner that can be verified with data

Leading participants to select an appropriate focus area and goal is not usually a difficult task. Through brainstorming learning objectives and listing responsibilities, participants have a variety of choices for their projects.

Session 1 of the eight staff development sessions is devoted to brainstorming interest or growth areas and defining responsibilities. Session 2 opens with identifying the focus, and then moves into the next stage of planning. This chapter will deal with brainstorming and identifying the focus. When a session addresses more than one stage, the mini-lesson will be presented with the stage to which it best applies. This is the case with Session 2, and the mini-lesson will be addressed in another chapter.

SESSION 1

Session	First 15 Minutes	Next 30 Minutes	Body of Session 90 Minutes	Final 15 Minutes
1	Introductions, Climate Setting	Orientation to Model	Brainstorm Interest/Growth Areas, Define Responsibilities	Individual Reflection

Introductions, Climate Setting, and Orientation to the Model

After opening the first session with introductions and creating a light atmosphere, the next order of business is to orient the group to the staff development model. Simply, they are to understand that they will plan, implement, and evaluate a project related to their professional roles. While it may take a couple of weeks for participants to understand that they truly are in control of all the decisions, they seem to grasp the project concept fairly quickly.

Brainstorming Interest/Growth Areas

Before moving to the learning plan, the first step is to help each person determine exactly what interests him or her and what his or her growth areas are. Knowles (1975) used a "Worksheet for Stating Learning Objectives" that I found particularly useful for brainstorming (see Figure 4.1). It can be adapted to focus brainstorming on the types of learning desired of participants. For example, if classroom research is preferred to general content development, prompts might include, "I would like to learn how _____ impacts student achievement in _____ (content area)," or, "I want to experiment with strategies to increase student proficiency with the following skills: _____." I included a column on the worksheet for "Background Student Achievement Data/Rationale for Interest" as a focus for the ultimate purpose of education and professional development: improved student achievement.

The prompts on the left side of the worksheet initiate brainstorming for development of knowledge, understanding, skill, a product, and values and attitudes. It is not necessary for participants to generate seven responses for each prompt; I suggest just writing as many as they can.

Behavioral Aspect	Topics for Study	Background Student Achievement Data/Rationale for Interest
I want to develop my *knowledge* about:	1. 2. 3. 4. 5. 6. 7.	
I would like to better *understand:*	1. 2. 3. 4. 5. 6. 7.	
I want to develop *skill* in:	1. 2. 3. 4. 5. 6. 7.	
I would like to *develop or create:*	1. 2. 3. 4. 5. 6. 7.	
I would like to develop *an appreciation or value* of:	1. 2. 3. 4. 5. 6. 7.	

Figure 4.1   Worksheet for Stating Learning Objectives

SOURCE: Adapted from Knowles (1975).

At times, a response may apply to more than one prompt, and it is fine to write the response more than once. The purpose of the exercise is to consider a number of interests and growth areas, so that a variety of choices is available.

The right side of the worksheet is for considering student achievement data related to interests and growth areas. Typically educators consider "data" that which is gathered from standardized test scores. For the purposes of this model, "data" can include any information that describes the performance of students—academic or behavioral. Examples could include

- State or national tests
- Local benchmark assessments
- Classroom grades as a whole
- Classroom grades on specific types of assignments or assessments
- Discipline and attendance information
- Demographic information such as poverty statistics in relation to academic performance
- Student proficiency with concepts within the curriculum

Before attending this session, teachers should be familiar with data concerning their students. If they are not, the facilitator should incorporate time for participants to review student achievement data in advance of brainstorming and goal setting.

Learning Plan: Defining Responsibilities

After completing the brainstorming worksheet, the next step in identifying the focus is to define responsibilities. This is done on the first page of the learning plan. To do this, participants generate lists of professional duties in the areas of organizational goals, instruction, administration, management/discipline, and "other." They can write in bulleted lists, phrases, sentences, or any other manner they choose throughout the plan.

There are often questions about what should be listed under each of the areas. It is important to stress that there is no right or wrong answer; participants simply write what they perceive their responsibilities to be.

At this point, the facilitator should emphasize that meeting school and district goals, particularly in relation to student achievement, is part of each person's responsibilities. Organizational goals should be reviewed with the group. I suggest providing each person with a copy of the goals for reference. If there is any confusion about the roles participants play in addressing these specific goals, the facilitator or school administrator should clarify expectations. The range of development options is vastly different for a broad school goal, such as "Increase student achievement on standardized tests," compared to a refined goal, like "Increase reading comprehension through strategy instruction, use of guided reading and graphic organizers, and contextual application of vocabulary." In order to merge teacher and school goals, teachers must clearly understand their role in addressing whole school issues.

After completing the brainstorming activity and listing responsibilities, the first session comes to a close. Participants are charged with selecting a focus that is both an interest or growth area and is associated with a professional responsibility tied to student achievement. In Session 2 they will set a goal and describe how it aligns with school and district goals and how it impacts student achievement.

Position: Participant A

RESPONSIBILITIES

Organizational Goals

School

    Improve student achievement in math and English on the graduation test; improve graduation rate

District

    Improve student achievement on standardized tests

Instruction

    Algebra: one semester class
    Math Concepts I: Problem Solving
    Math Concepts II: Probability and Statistics
    Give content-based writing assignments once a week, grade for content
    Give content-based reading assignments once a week, give purpose for reading
    Vary strategies for instruction

Administration

    Give required tests, benchmark assessments

Management/Discipline

    Enter grades in electronic grade book regularly, address student misbehavior

Other

    Plan with math department, write unit and lesson plans

Individual Reflection

The final activity of the session is individual reflection. Typically each person should write three thoughts or responses associated with the program or his or her learning. Along with the responses, to prompt deeper reflection they are to include examples to illustrate their points. I use the following prompt on a single sheet of 8 ½ × 11 paper:

> Reflect in a written journal entry at least three thoughts in order to explain your beliefs, actions, and experience with the staff development program. Please provide specific examples to illustrate your points.

Position: 6th-Grade Language Arts

RESPONSIBILITIES

Organizational Goals

School

 Increase reading and math scores on the spring standardized test

District

 To become a world-class school system by providing quality instruction, increasing student achievement, and making sure students are prepared for college or work

Instruction

 Reading/literature, writing, speaking/persuasive speech, behavior modification, responsibility and respect, technology incorporation, love of reading

 Increase reading scores on state test as part of school goal

Administration

 Student Support Team meetings, parent conferences, team meetings, grade level meetings

Management/Discipline

 Hall duty, lunch duty, detention, classroom management and discipline, grades

Other

 Beta Club sponsor, vertical team member

While facilitators do not respond in writing to what each person has written, they should address any concerns expressed by learners as appropriate in the group setting or one-on-one with individuals. It is critical that participants be assured that they are in control of their learning, that there is no right or wrong approach, and that they will be supported along the way.

SESSION 2

Session 2 addresses all four broad phases of the learning plan: identifying the focus, defining the problem, planning for self-directed study, and self-directed study. Since each of these four phases is discussed in its own chapter, portions of Session 2 will be addressed across four different chapters. Only Session 2 activities leading through "identifying focus" will be discussed in this chapter.

Session	First 15 Minutes	Next 30 Minutes	Body of Session 90 Minutes	Final 15 Minutes
2	Group Reflection	*Learning Plan:* Identifying Focus, Defining the Problem, Planning for Self-Directed Study, Self-Directed Study (Research/Data Gathering Section) *Mini-Lesson:* Introduce Template for Evaluating Written Material	Individual Work Time	Individual Reflection

Group Reflection

Session 2 opens with each person stating aloud to the group where he or she is in the process of selecting a goal. The purpose of opening each session with reflection is to create an atmosphere of collaboration and to reduce anxiety. By hearing that others are often having the same successes and difficulties, individuals realize their own challenges are normal. As well, members of the group are inclined to offer support to one another after this activity, even when working on different topics and projects.

Learning Plan: Identifying Focus

The first stage in planning the project occurs in Session 2. In this stage, "identifying focus," an interest or growth area is selected, rationale is given for selecting the area, and the direct relationship to professional responsibilities, student achievement, and school and district goals is described.

In completing this part of the plan, it is important that the facilitator help participants connect their focus areas to student achievement and school and district goals. Specifically, the facilitator should assist participants to select appropriate data that describe current student achievement. If specific classroom or other student achievement data were listed with the focus area during brainstorming, this would be the place to describe them.

For example, if a fifth-grade teacher pulled the standardized data for each of her students and realized content and organization of writing were group deficits, she could use these data as the rationale for learning about writing strategies. This section for background data and providing a rationale for learning will be most difficult for learners choosing to develop their knowledge of content. While it is easy enough to say that one is learning new information, connecting that learning to student achievement will

Position: Participant A

IDENTIFYING FOCUS

Area of interest or targeted change/improvement
Activating thinking strategies

Reason for interest/concern regarding this area
Need to get students involved in the lesson more quickly

How does this interest/concern relate to your responsibilities?
I have to teach math and increase student achievement. This hits both.

Describe how development in this area will improve student achievement. Include background data regarding this area. Describe desired student achievement outcomes that can be verified with data.
I want to use "starters" to review previous lessons or give students a problem that ties to the new lesson. If students buy into the starters and get interested early in the class period, I don't have to spend as much time getting them engaged later. We can cover more material, so our benchmark scores at the midpoint should be good. Students' grades in the class should go up after we start using the activating thinking strategies.

How does this relate to schoolwide and systemwide goals?
One goal is to increase student achievement in math. If I get students engaged in learning they should achieve more.

Position: In-School Suspension Coordinator

IDENTIFYING FOCUS

Area of interest or targeted change/improvement
Computer literacy. Create record-keeping methods using Microsoft Access. I have 0% knowledge regarding creating forms, spreadsheets, and data reports.

Reason for interest/concern regarding this area

1. *Self-improvement*

2. *Can communicate more effectively with administration, counselors, and peers about students placed in ISS*

3. *Use the data to make recommendations for intervention with most pervasive schoolwide problems*

How does this interest/concern relate to your responsibilities?

I was told I should keep records and statistics on students who are placed in the ISS room. When asked for the data, I want to be able to quickly and effectively give up-to-the-minute information.

Describe how development in this area will improve student achievement. Include background data regarding this area. Describe desired student achievement outcomes that can be verified with data.

My records indicate that fighting and gang-related posturing are predominant behaviors in our school. By knowing who comes to ISS and why, the school can come up with programs to address the most widespread problems. If students remain in the regular classroom, they will learn more. I would like to see a reduction in the number of students assigned to ISS, especially for fighting and gang-related behaviors.

How does this relate to schoolwide and systemwide goals?

The school wants to decrease the number of disciplinary incidents. Our school has the highest rate of disciplinary referrals in the district.

be difficult. How does a teacher measure how students perform before he or she learns the new content and after he or she learns and applies the new content? It can be proven that the teacher grew—an accountability measure for the program—but how can student achievement be measured? It is important to remember that effective professional development impacts student achievement, and unless distinct connections to students and the school are made, an important outcome of professional development is lost.

CONCLUSION

At this point, the first stage of the learning plan is complete. An area of focus has been identified and connected to student achievement and school and district goals. Participants have engaged in the first individual and group reflections, and a climate of collaboration has been established. If done well, the foundation has been laid for an effective learning experience. The next stage of the learning plan is defining the problem, and its focus is setting a specific goal for the project.

5

Working From the Learning Plan

Defining the Problem

In this stage of the learning plan, "defining the problem," the focus is on setting a specific goal for the project. It is important that each individual select only one or two goals, and that the goals be described in objective terms. It should be very clear what goal attainment will look like, so that a person unfamiliar with the project could determine whether or not the goal was met. This stage is completed during Session 2.

SESSION 2

Session	First 15 Minutes	Next 30 Minutes	Body of Session 90 Minutes	Final 15 Minutes
2	Group Reflection	*Learning Plan:* Identifying Focus, Defining the Problem, Planning for Self-Directed Study, Self-Directed Study (Research/Data Gathering Section) *Mini-Lesson:* Introduce Template for Evaluating Written Material	Individual Work Time	Individual Reflection

Learning Plan: Defining the Problem

In "defining the problem," participants list goals they hope to accomplish as a result of study in the focus area, identify processes for assessing pre- and post-project levels of knowledge and skill, identify indicators of success in achieving project goals, and note how student achievement will be measured.

Position: Participant A

DEFINING THE PROBLEM

List the goals you hope to accomplish as a result of developing your knowledge and skills in the focus area. Phrase the outcomes as observable behaviors.

- *Students are actively engaged in learning.*
- *Students use terms related to math. (Working with vocabulary before a lesson is an activating thinking strategy.)*

Identify the process(es) you will use to assess *your* pre- and post-project levels of performance, behavior, thinking, understanding, and so on. Be certain these assessments correlate with the outcomes you hope to achieve as a result of study in the focus area.

Right now I do not know any activating thinking strategies. I will assess my learning by how many strategies I use in my classes.

Identify indicators of success that demonstrate achievement of study goals.

I will observe students using the terms in class and when they work with peers. Student achievement will be higher.

Identify the methods you will use to demonstrate the impact your study will have on student achievement. What data will you collect to measure change?

1. *I will look at benchmark test scores to see if students learned information we studied in class.*

2. *I will compare student grades on tests before I started using the A.T.S. and after using the A.T.S.*

Selecting a Goal

Again, each person should select one, or no more than two, goals. In deciding exactly what to do, participants should take into account that the program lasts for eight weeks. The first session is devoted to brainstorming and defining responsibilities, and the last session is set aside for sharing projects. That leaves only six sessions and a total of nine hours for individual work time. A participant can certainly choose to work on the

---

Position: Gifted Coordinator

DEFINING THE PROBLEM

List the goals you hope to accomplish as a result of developing your knowledge and skills in the focus area. Phrase the outcomes as observable behaviors.

I want to create a program of directed study and pull-out seminars for gifted students.

Identify the process(es) you will use to assess *your* pre- and post-project levels of performance, behavior, thinking, understanding, and so on. Be certain these assessments correlate with the outcomes you hope to achieve as a result of study in the focus area.

There is no program currently. I do not know how to implement directed study or pull-out seminars. If I have learned how directed study and seminars work, and I have started a program at our school, I will have achieved my goal.

Identify indicators of success that demonstrate achievement of study goals.

A functional, sustained gifted program including directed study and pull-out seminars.

Identify the methods you will use to demonstrate the impact your study will have on student achievement. What data will you collect to measure change?

Through individual and small-group arrangements, gifted students will do research and projects that stretch them academically according to their specific talents. An inventory of what they know and can do, in relation to the topic studied, will be taken before beginning the project and after it is completed.

---

project outside of the staff development sessions, but this is not required. Whatever goal is selected, it should be practical given the amount of time one intends to devote.

Learners should be encouraged to "stretch" themselves. For example, a high school social studies teacher may have researched idiosyncratic facets of the Civil War. To pursue another similar micro-study will not grow the learner, per se. But to study instructional delivery formats (lecture, role play, multimedia presentations) in comparison with achievement of various student populations or students of various learning styles would not only develop analytical reflection, but would also elevate the teacher's overall instructional practice. A much greater potential for individual growth is present when learners select personally challenging goals.

Just as with student learning, goals aligned with higher levels of Bloom's Taxonomy draw adults into more advanced types of learning.

When teachers evaluate the effectiveness of their practices in relation to student achievement, or design an instructional response to analysis of data on student performance, professional growth is more significant. Goals designed to solve problems and apply learned concepts are qualitatively superior to goals directed toward simply collecting and organizing information. This is not to say that deepening of content knowledge is an unacceptable goal, just that it should be done to become a better instructor of the material and not as a tangential exploration into a favored topic. Facilitators should devote time at this stage to helping learners choose goals that promote real professional growth, rather than simply writing a goal that describes a project activity.

Pre- and Post-Project Assessment of Participants' Learning

The next section of the plan, pre-project and post-project assessment, is one of the most difficult for participants to complete. The primary confusion is in determining *how* to assess their own pre-project and post-project levels of performance. Generally, classroom teachers want to use student achievement data here. While student data may support that a goal was attained, the pre-project and post-project assessment is to measure the *participant's growth* across the staff development program. This is how accountability for individualized learning is addressed.

When determining pre-project and post-project levels of performance, the assessment should match what is to be changed or improved. For example, if a teacher wants to implement strategies that would increase the overall reading comprehension of her students, then using student data on reading comprehension would be one form of pre-project assessment. But, in addition, she should list and account for the types of strategies she used to address reading comprehension before beginning her project. Demonstrating an increase in the number of strategies used shows development on the teacher's part, while an increase in students' reading comprehension shows that the strategies implemented were successful.

There are other cases, though, where participants want to increase their knowledge base or skill level within a particular area. In a case like this, simply defining the pre-project level of knowledge or skill would be sufficient. For example, in Chapter 4, the In-School Suspension teacher wanted to learn how to use a spreadsheet program. He had no prior experience using such a program, and to state that he had no understanding of the program provides a specific starting point to which progress can be compared. Devising a more complicated assessment in this situation is not practical or necessary.

Indicators of Success: Participants' Visions of Desired Outcomes

Moving beyond establishment of pre-project knowledge and skill, generating indicators of success leads participants to envision the end result they would like to achieve. An indicator of success not only establishes what goal attainment will look like, but it sets the standard of achievement the person hopes to reach. There should be a gap between the pre-project level of performance and the indicator of success at the beginning of the project. If there is no gap, then it will be difficult to demonstrate growth across the course of the program.

The example of the gifted teacher illustrates the difference between a goal and an indicator of achievement. The goal was to create a program, and the indicator of success was that the program would be implemented and functioning. On a smaller scale, a high school math teacher wanted to increase the number of days he used collaborative work groups in his classes. The goal was to increase use, and the indicator of achievement was that instead of using collaborative groups one or two times in a two-week period, he would use them at least five times in the same time frame. Further, he noted as an indicator of success that assessment of collaborative work would include mastery of objectives and student interaction. Clearly, the standards the teachers established for success went beyond simply meeting the initial goals they established.

Measuring Student Achievement Resulting From Participant Learning

Finally, participants are to identify methods they will use to demonstrate the impact of their learning on student achievement. Although common assessment of student achievement relies on annually derived standardized scores, for the purposes of evaluating project effectiveness, learners should consider not only broad scale data, but also the spectrum of data sources. For example, locally developed tests of achievement, such as benchmark assessments, provide excellent pre- and post-intervention levels of knowledge and skill. As well, teacher-made assessments with identical question formats, levels of difficulty, and numbers of questions can indicate the effect of instructor changes on student learning. Similar assignments completed before and after an intervention was applied can show the impact of change in a particular area. Rubrics can be used to demonstrate advancement in student performance and skill as a result of teacher implementation of new strategy. Participants should be creative in identifying a measure that shows a direct impact on student skill development and content mastery as a result of the educator's learning and its application.

For example, if a teacher wants to learn about and incorporate reading comprehension strategies into her high school science course, she should identify types of data that would show a difference in student achievement before and after teaching the strategies. She could elect to use a standard format for evaluating students on readings, such as seven questions soliciting clearly stated facts and three critical thinking questions that would require comprehension of the material for a correct response. By using this same evaluation format before and after implementing the strategies, the teacher could assess whether or not students comprehended factual and implied information at a higher rate as a result of the strategies implemented, as well as assess which strategies led to a higher rate of correct responses. Clearly, in this case, use of standardized data collected once a year or overall classroom grades would be ineffective to determine the impact of the specific strategies used on student achievement.

If selection or creation of appropriate data collection tools is done well, the participant, the students, the school, and the district benefit from the professional development program. Clear data are gathered regarding the effectiveness of specific teacher learning and its direct application in the classroom. If appropriate data collection tools are not selected or created, the effectiveness of specific strategies and knowledge applied in the participant's role cannot be determined.

CONCLUSION

Defining the problem sets the direction of the self-directed learning project. A goal is established. The means by which to measure progress is determined. And finally, each person sets the standard for what he or she considers a successful outcome and how student achievement will be demonstrated. The next stage of the project is to plan for self-directed study.

6

Working From the Learning Plan

Planning for Self-Directed Study

The third stage of the learning plan is "planning for self-directed study." Still in Session 2, participants decide whether they will work alone or with others, how they will organize information, and in what time frame they want to complete the project. Overall, this stage is about organizing oneself to begin work.

SESSION 2

Session	First 15 Minutes	Next 30 Minutes	Body of Session 90 Minutes	Final 15 Minutes
2	Group Reflection	*Learning Plan:* Identifying Focus, Defining the Problem, Planning for Self-Directed Study, Self-Directed Study (Research/Data Gathering Section) *Mini-Lesson:* Introduce Template for Evaluating Written Material	Individual Work Time	Individual Reflection

Learning Plan: Planning for Self-Directed Study

Planning for self-directed study is meant to focus learners on the minutiae of organization. Failing to account at the outset for how learning will take place and according to what schedule will result in tasks taking longer to complete. As well, the end of the staff development program could creep up on learners surprisingly quickly and catch them unable to complete or organize learning into a format useful in their roles. Only a small amount of time at this point is necessary to address this potential problem.

Mode for Conducting Study

Planning for self-directed study begins with selecting the mode for study: self-instruction, cooperative learning, team learning, or other. Self-instruction simply means that the individual will work alone to gather information, as opposed to working with a partner or group. It does not preclude the person from interviewing others or asking for assistance. Cooperative learning groups generally comprise a small number of people who work toward a single goal, and all members contribute equally to all parts of the project. Team learning is an offshoot of cooperative learning. The team works together to develop a base of information on the topic, but thereafter each member independently pursues an interest area related to the topic. "Other" provides for any other methods a person might use to gather information, such as by attending a seminar or conference.

Organizing Data and Resources

After deciding how to gather information, participants next select a method for organizing data and resources. This exercise is fairly easy for most. For convenience, each person should consider the ways he or she will most likely get information, and then choose an organizational tool that matches. For example, if information will generally be collected from the Internet, an electronic folder may be most convenient. But if conventional paper copies of materials will be used, either paper folders or a notebook may be most useful. Likewise, if the person will be taking notes at seminars or conferences, spiral notebooks come in handy.

Setting the Time Frame for Completing Project Components

The next section, determining the timeline for project completion, is misunderstood more than any other part of the plan. This is a section for listing dates. Many times participants will begin to write in plans for parts of the project, and shortly confusion sets in. They realize their responses do not seem to flow with the pieces of the plan they have already completed. The facilitator should carefully monitor responses here to make sure the group is on track.

Guidance for setting dates will need to be provided. It helps to refer the group back to the program agenda. The agenda provides a general guide

---

Position: Participant A

PLANNING FOR SELF-DIRECTED STUDY

Mode for conducting study

  X Self-Instruction

  ____ Cooperative Learning (Group study)
Group Members _____

  ____ Team Learning (Group study for core material and self-instruction for corollary info.) Group Members _____

  ____ Other _____

What organizational method will you utilize to organize your data and resources?

  X 3-ring binder or portfolio   ____ Spiral notebook/journal

  ____ Folders/filing system   ____ Multimedia

  ____ Electronic format   ____ Other _____

Define the timeframe in which you will complete the project.

Entire project: *by November 15*

Project components:

  Pre-project assessment *by September 1*

  Summary/interpretation of pre-project assessment *by September 1*

  Research/data gathering *Ongoing starting September 2*

  Interpretation of research/data gathering *by October 1*

  Translating new knowledge/skills into a plan to meet goals *by October 1*

  Implementation of plan to meet goals *No later than October 15*

  Post-project assessment *by November 15*

  Summary/interpretation of post-study assessment *by November 15*

---

for finishing projects within the time frame of the staff development program. It is important to clarify for participants that they may be ahead of the group in completing some stages of the plan and behind the group in completing other stages. More important than completing each stage according the agenda is working steadily to complete the project by the end of the program. If a project cannot be completed by the conclusion of the staff development program, the participant should note which parts of the project will be finished, or alter the goal.

Position: Special Education
Teacher: Emotional Behavioral Disorders

PLANNING FOR SELF-DIRECTED STUDY

Mode for conducting study

_____ Self-Instruction

__X__ Cooperative Learning (Group study)

Group Members *Troy, Sally*

_____ Team Learning (Group study for core material and self-instruction for corollary info.) Group Members _____

_____ Other _____

What organizational method will you utilize to organize your data and resources?

__X__ 3-ring binder or portfolio   _____ Spiral notebook/journal

__X__ Folders/filing system   _____ Multimedia

__X__ Electronic format   _____ Other _____

Define the timeframe in which you will complete the project.

8 weeks (8 sessions)

Entire project:

I intend to finish this project by the time the staff development program ends. If I do not finish by then, I will be finished by the end of the semester.

Project components:

Pre-project assessment *February 6*

Summary/interpretation of pre-project assessment *February 13*

Research/data gathering *February 20*

Interpretation of research/data gathering *February 20*

Translating new knowledge/skills into a plan to meet goals *February 27*

Implementation of plan to meet goals *February 27 or March 6*

Post-project assessment *March 27*

Summary/interpretation of post-study assessment *March 27*

Revisiting the Timelines

After setting the time frame, it is important to revisit it each week. After beginning the project, time seems to pass very quickly. Individuals may find that goals need to be refined or broadened based upon what they can accomplish in the time given. Adjustment of goals due to the time frame is typical, as participants come to grasp what can be accomplished in eight sessions. My experience has been that about one quarter to one half of a group reduces or expands a project based on what they discover can be accomplished in the time frame.

CONCLUSION

Planning for self-directed study concludes the preparatory stages of the learning plan. Each individual should know if learning will be conducted independently or with a group. A method for organizing information has been selected. And, finally, a time frame for completing the project has been set. The participants are ready to begin the final and most lengthy stage, self-directed study.

7

Working From the Learning Plan

Self-Directed Study

The last and longest stage of the plan, "self-directed study," commences implementation of the learning plan. Self-directed study is broken into substages, each of which includes a variety of concepts and activities. These substages are completed in Sessions 2 through 8 and incorporate the following: *research/data gathering, pre-project assessment, summary/interpretation of pre-project assessment, interpretation of research/data gathering, translating new knowledge/skills into plan to meet goals, implementation of plan to meet goals, post-project assessment*, and *summary/interpretation of post-project assessment*.

SESSION 2

Session	First 15 Minutes	Next 30 Minutes	Body of Session 90 Minutes	Final 15 Minutes
2	Group Reflection	*Learning Plan:* Identifying Focus, Defining the Problem, Planning for Self-Directed Study, Self-Directed Study (Research/Data Gathering Section) *Mini-Lesson:* Introduce Template for Evaluating Written Material	Individual Work Time	Individual Reflection

The final activities of Session 2, those related to "self-directed study," will be described in this chapter. As well, the remaining six sessions of the basic staff development program, all devoted to "self-directed study," will be presented.

Learning Plan: Self-Directed Study

During self-directed study, the learning project is actually conducted. Substages of self-directed study occur in three basic phases: data gathering, translating knowledge into an action plan, and assessing learning. Each substage is composed of a variety of steps. They will be described according to the sessions in which they occur.

Research and Data Gathering

The first phase of self-directed study includes research and data gathering, pre-project assessment, summary and interpretation of pre-project assessment, and interpretation of research and data gathering. The last piece of the learning plan completed during Session 2 is research and data gathering. This includes listing topics and key words to use in study of the focus area, identifying methods for gathering information (e.g., professional journals and books, online research, observations, etc.), and identifying areas where assistance may be needed in data gathering.

Position: Participant A

SELF-DIRECTED STUDY

Research/Data Gathering

List topics and key words to be utilized in study of your focus area.

- *Engaging students*
- *Lesson openers or activities*

Methods you will utilize to gather information about your focus area.

_X_ Magazine and journal articles   _X_ Online research

___ Professional books   ___ Multimedia (video, tape recording, etc.)

___ Other professional documents   ___ Expert resources

___ Interviews and surveys   ___ Others' observations of me

___ Observation of others   _X_ Other *Discussions with other teachers*

In gathering information about my focus area, I may need help with:
Finding some "proven" activating thinking strategies

Position: Related Vocational Instructor–High School

SELF-DIRECTED STUDY

Research/Data Gathering

List topics and key words to be utilized in study of your focus area.

Assessment, vocational, technical, careers

Methods you will utilize to gather information about your focus area.

_X_ Magazine and journal articles   _X_ Online research

___ Professional books   ___ Multimedia (video, tape recording, etc.)

___ Other professional documents   _X_ Expert resources

_X_ Interviews and surveys   ___ Others' observations of me

_X_ Observation of others   ___ Other _____

In gathering information about my focus area, I may need help with:
   Gathering contact information for other schools that have RVI teachers—I can talk with those teachers about the types of vocational assessments that are available.

The *research/data gathering* stage is straightforward. It focuses the search on particular terms and resources. The final question, "In gathering information about my focus area, I may need help with," prompts individuals to consider difficulties they may face. By identifying these at the onset of the project, participants can plan for the help they need before experiencing a barrier to progress.

Mini-Lesson

After completing the *research/data gathering* stage, the final group activity of Session 2 is a mini-lesson. This first mini-lesson is simply an introduction to the Template for Evaluating Written Material (Figure 7.1) and a review of types of written material (Figure 7.2).

The template is a tool for summarizing information and determining its relevance to the project. Use of the template is at the participants' discretion. Types of written material are discussed, and emphasis is placed on selecting quality resources when gathering information. The facilitator should share examples of each type of written material. Explanation of types and common examples I use are included in Figure 7.2.

```
┌──────────────────────────────────────────────────────────────────┐
│                    EVALUATING WRITTEN MATERIAL                     │
│                                                                    │
│   TITLE:                                                           │
│                                                                    │
│   AUTHOR:                                                          │
│                                                                    │
│   SOURCE:                                                          │
│                                                                    │
│   DATE / VOLUME / ISSUE:                                           │
│                                                                    │
│   TYPE:      Research-Quantitative   Research-Qualitative   Not Research │
│                                                                    │
│   Book      Journal Article         Newspaper Article      Web Info │
│                                                                    │
│   Other _____                           │
│                                                                    │
│   Topic:                                                           │
│                                                                    │
│   Summary:                                                         │
│                                                                    │
│   Implications for Project:                                        │
└──────────────────────────────────────────────────────────────────┘
```

Figure 7.1   Template for Evaluating Written Material

SOURCE: Adapted from Calhoun (1994).

In Session 3, during the mini-lesson, the group will practice using the template.

Individual Work Time

The remainder of Session 2 is devoted to individual work and a concluding individual reflection. All participants are asked to remain in the presence of the facilitator during this time. There are two reasons for this: to provide support as needed to individuals, and to ensure that participants engage in appropriate activities during this time. If an optimal location has been selected for the staff development sessions, all adults should have ample room to work and access to computers and online resources. A gentle reminder to all participants that loud noise and distractions impede the learning of others should set the expectation of professional respect. To reiterate a prior caution, facilitators should gingerly set these expectations so that the assembled adults do not feel their personal respect or control has been compromised.

Individual Reflection

As in Session 1, the final activity of Session 2 is individual reflection. Each person is to write at least three thoughts or responses associated with the program or his or her learning. Along with responses, he or she is to include examples to illustrate his or her points. It will still be necessary at this point to assure participants they are in control of their learning, that there is no right or wrong approach, and that they will be supported along

TYPES OF WRITTEN MATERIAL

RESEARCH–QUANTITATIVE

Quantitative research deals with numbers and statistics. With these studies, terms such as *significance, correlation, variables, control group,* and *conditions* are used in reporting results. Quantitative research deals with any number of topics.

MacMillan, R. (1999). Influences of workplace conditions on teachers' job satisfaction. *Journal of Educational Research, 93,* 39–47.

RESEARCH–QUALITATIVE

Qualitative research deals with exploring the lived experiences of human beings. Generally, these studies explore those experiences in detail. Terms such as *coding, theme, subjectivity,* and *member check* are used in qualitative studies.

Blase, J., & Blase, J.R. (1994). *Empowering teachers: What successful principals do.* Thousand Oaks, CA: Corwin Press.

NON-RESEARCH

Non-research includes anything that is not a study. Often these materials are informative, but they do not provide the proof of a study to support conclusions made. In some cases, articles and books may be based on research, but they are not classified as research themselves.

Jensen, E. (1996). *Brain-based learning.* Del Mar, CA: Turning Point.

BOOK

This is self-explanatory. Try to discern integrity of the information published.

JOURNAL ARTICLE

Journals are serial publications that are published on a regular basis. Articles published in a journal usually fall under a particular theme; for example, *Educational Leadership* focuses on topics of general interest to school leaders. Some journals require a peer review before articles are accepted for publication. These journals are generally considered to be of a higher caliber.

Sherin, M. (2000). Viewing teaching on videotape. *Educational Leadership, 57,* 36–38.

NEWSPAPER ARTICLE

This is self-explanatory. Try to discern integrity of the information published.

WEB INFORMATION

This consists of any information published on the Internet. Some journal articles are published online. They are still considered journal articles. When relying on information published on the Web, try to ensure that the information is reliable and delivered by a trustworthy source.

Nunley, K. (2000, April). Keeping pace with today's quick brains. *Brains.org* [Online serial]. Available: www.brains.org

Figure 7.2 Types of Written Material

the way. And it is of utmost importance that the facilitator not make choices or decisions for participants, so that self-direction in learning is nurtured.

SESSION 3

Session	First 15 Minutes	Next 30 Minutes	Body of Session 90 Minutes	Final 15 Minutes
3	Group Reflection	*Learning Plan:* Self-Directed Study (Pre-Project Assessment, Summary/ Interpretation of Pre-Project Assessment Sections) *Mini-Lesson:* Critically Evaluating Information Using Template from Session 2; Demonstrate How to Use Online Databases to Gather Information	Individual Work Time	Individual Reflection

Session 3 work is devoted to reflections, assessing and interpreting the *participants'* knowledge and skill before beginning the projects, and individual work.

Group Reflection

In the first 15 minutes of Session 3, group members give an update on their progress and state their plans for individual work. This is a time of discourse and support. It is during this portion of the session that learners come to understand their challenges are part of the self-directed process and not a reflection of inadequacy. It is important that the facilitator encourage learners in their efforts and remind them barriers to progress can be expected.

Learning Plan: Self-Directed Learning

The next sections of the learning plan are for assessing participants' beginning knowledge and skill. Student data may also be included to set a beginning point of student achievement that is more focused than the possibly general data given as background information or rationale for the project. The data related at this point sets the stage for learning, verifying the direction chosen is indeed a growth area.

Pre-Project Assessment

Pre-project assessment simply involves listing the results of the pre-project assessment so that a baseline for learning or implementing the project is established. The assessment can be formal or informal, qualitative or quantitative, as the learner deems appropriate to measure project goals. This assessment was established in Session 2 when the individual identified the goal and stated how pre- and post-project levels of his or her performance would be measured. In order to answer the prompts in this section, the pre-project assessment must have been conducted and results accumulated.

Position: Participant A

Pre-Project Assessment

List results of pre-study assessment.
I have not used activating thinking strategies, so I am starting from zero.
Summary/Interpretation of Pre-Project Assessment

Summarize the implications of pre-study assessment.
I need to do something to help students review what we have learned and keep the info fresh.

Did the results of the pre-study assessment validate or alter the focus of your interest or concern? Briefly explain.
I tested out one strategy to see how it would work. About 50% were more focused on the lesson. Between this and having no prior knowledge of the strategies my focus was validated. Students need to get engaged that quickly, and they need that review.

Is it necessary to refine your area of interest or concern? If yes, how will you modify your project?
No—on track

Position: Chorus Teacher

Pre-Project Assessment

List results of pre-study assessment.
I discovered there is no middle school choral program in our district, so this project is to find a body of information to convince the "decision makers" there should be one. There are many resources and articles on the importance of choral music for students and for keeping a program strong. It will be important to set a limit on the amount of information gathered, so I can move on to organizing it to make a case.
Summary/Interpretation of Pre-Project Assessment

(Continued)

(Continued)

> Summarize the implications of pre-study assessment.
>
> *The pre-study assessment was simply that there is no middle school choral program. I have found many interesting articles and helpful resources that I didn't even know existed. I think the resources may be helpful in persuading decision makers and parents of the value of a choral program. The main thrust of my research will be finding out who seems to make the final decisions on what is offered in our schools.*
>
> Did the results of the pre-study assessment validate or alter the focus of your interest or concern? Briefly explain.
>
> *I think that after looking at all the info available, interviews with district and school administrators will give me the most concrete information. Then I will decide where to concentrate my persuasion on the value of choral music.*
>
> Is it necessary to refine your area of interest or concern? If yes, how will you modify your project?
>
> *Yes, with the time given I will not be able to talk with as many other district music teachers as I would like. This will be another project to get us all on the same page.*

Summary and Interpretation of Pre-Project Assessment

During *summary/interpretation of pre-project assessment*, the learner summarizes the implications of the pre-study assessment, determines if study in the focus area is still appropriate, and then refines the project if necessary. This stage of the plan is the first reflective piece, and it prompts learners to assess the direction they have chosen. Participants should be reminded at this point, and throughout the program, that they retain the right to adjust their plans in response to learning.

Mini-Lesson

After completing sections of the learning plan related to pre-project assessment, the next activity in Session 3 is the mini-lesson. Using the Template for Evaluating Written Material introduced in Session 2, participants practice reviewing written information. The focus of the activity is on determining reliability of information presented and implications for individual projects. The facilitator provides various types of educational literature to participants for practice. After learners have reviewed and evaluated written material for about 10 minutes, group members share information about each piece and what led them to deem the piece reliable or unreliable as a source of information.

In the last few minutes of the mini-lesson, the facilitator should demonstrate how to use online search engines and databases for information gathering. Participants should be shown how to find journal articles and research-based publications. Often libraries and universities will have Internet research tools available to the general public. It would be wise to test any sites to be demonstrated just prior to this session, as Web resources can change, disappear, or become unavailable without notice.

Individual Work Time and Individual Reflections

As a transition to individual work time, participants can be given the option of searching the Internet for resources. The remainder of time in Session 3 is devoted to individual work time and individual reflections.

SESSION 4

Session	First 15 Minutes	Next 30 Minutes	Body of Session 90 Minutes	Final 15 Minutes
4	Group Reflection	Mini-Lesson: Basic Terminology of Qualitative and Quantitative Research	Individual Work Time	Individual Reflection

Time in Session 4 is allotted primarily for reflections, the mini-lesson, and individual work time.

Group Reflection

Session 4 opens with group reflection. After sharing progress and committing to activities for individual work time, participants should review their timelines for projects. This session marks the halfway point, and goals should be revisited. If it is necessary to broaden or refine a goal based upon the time left in the program, learners should be reminded adjustment of the plan is at their discretion.

Learning Plan: Self-Directed Study

During this session, no new parts of the learning plan are covered with the group. Some individuals may have fallen behind, and this is a good time to catch up. Others may have gathered a good deal of information and want to move ahead in the learning plan. The facilitator should support individual learners wherever they are in the process.

Mini-Lesson

The mini-lesson for Session 4 covers terminology of quantitative (Figure 7.3) and qualitative (Figure 7.4) research. The purpose of this lesson is to familiarize participants with vocabulary or concepts they may encounter during data gathering. During discussion of the terms, participants are encouraged to share examples from their own resources if they apply.

QUANTITATIVE RESEARCH TERMINOLOGY

Quantitative research is concerned with the testing of hypotheses, and results are reported in terms of statistics.

COMPARISON: Compares groups

RELATIONSHIP/CORRELATION: Refers to relationships between variables. A positive, or direct, relationship indicates the group under study changes in the same manner as the item against which it is being compared. A negative, or inverse, relationship indicates the group under study changes, but in an opposite manner from the item against which it is compared.

VARIABLES: Components of the study that are isolated as the foci. The dependent variable is manipulated, while the independent variable remains constant.

INTERVENTION: A change that is applied to the research situation and subsequently studied.

HYPOTHESIS: Researcher's predicted finding of the study; is testable by manipulating variables.

NULL HYPOTHESIS: When the intervention or research indicates no difference or relationship.

STANDARD DEVIATION: The typical distance scores are from the mean.

VARIANCE: The average amount scores vary from the mean.

PROBABILITY: The degree of likelihood statistical data resulting from research are accurate.

SIGNIFICANCE: Statistical significance indicates the degree of relationship or result of intervention is greater than what would be expected to naturally occur.

TYPICAL DATA: Mean, median, mode, ratios, correlation, standard deviation, variance, probability, significance

---

Figure 7.3 Quantitative Research Terminology

SOURCE: Adapted from Schnitjer (1994).

QUALITATIVE RESEARCH TERMINOLOGY

Qualitative research is concerned with understanding human behaviors, beliefs, and perceptions, and most often it is reported in a narrative format.

METHODS: Procedures used to gather and analyze data

METHODOLOGY: Plan of action, design, or process behind the choice and use of particular methods

THEORETICAL PERSPECTIVE: Philosophy behind the methodology

EPISTEMOLOGY: The larger theory from which the philosophy, or theoretical perspective, is derived

ETHNOGRAPHY: Study of a person or persons from within their environment

CASE STUDY: Study of a particular case or individual

PHENOMENOLOGY: Study of the structure of a particular phenomenon, such as an anger episode

GROUNDED THEORY: Discovery and development of theory, rather than approaching research from a prior theoretical framework such as feminism

SUBJECTIVITIES: The experiences, beliefs, and perceptions a researcher brings to a study

TYPICAL DATA: Interviews, participant narrative accounts, observation and field notes, journal responses, archives

---

Figure 7.4 Qualitative Research Terminology

SOURCE: Adapted from Roulston (2001).

Individual Work Time and Individual Reflection

The final activities of Session 4 are individual work time and individual reflection. By this point in the program, participants should have a clear idea of what they will be able to accomplish. Work should be efficient and targeted. Most have taken ownership of their learning, and other than intermittent support, they should be gaining momentum.

SESSION 5

Session	First 15 Minutes	Next 30 Minutes	Body of Session 90 Minutes	Final 15 Minutes
5	Group Reflection	*Learning Plan:* Self-Directed Study (Interpretation of Research/Data Gathering, Translating New Knowledge/ Skills into Plan to Meet Goals Sections)	Individual Work Time	Individual Reflection

Session 5 marks movement into the second half of the professional development program. It would be wise for participants to take stock of their progress in relation to the timeline and goals previously set.

Group Reflection

Session 5 opens with group reflection and commitment to activities for individual work time. By this time, learners should be fairly clear and focused in the tasks chosen to complete goals. Due to the increased comfort with the program and camaraderie developed among the group, reflections may be more detailed and paired with reflective comments. As well, they may take more time than in earlier sessions.

Learning Plan: Self-Directed Study

Now participants move into completion of the next sections of the learning plan. Work during Session 5 is focused on interpreting what has been learned for use in participants' roles. Through *interpretation of research/data gathering,* the learner summarizes the most significant findings of study in the focus area, and then discusses opinions regarding the information gathered. This then transitions into the second phase of "self-directed learning," *translating new knowledge/skills into a plan to meet goals.*

Position: Participant A

Interpretation of Research/Data Gathering

Summarize the most significant findings of your research/data gathering as they relate to your focus area. (What important points do the data reveal? What patterns or trends are noted? How do data from various sources compare and contrast? Do any correlations seem important?)

The major important point revealed was how much the review problems helped the students maintain understanding of topics. I saw this on the benchmark test results. From day to day in the classroom I can get a feel for who is going to struggle with the new topic and who understands before a true introduction of the lesson happens. This allows me a chance to pair them for the day. That has proven very helpful. The students respond that it has helped.

Discuss your inferences/feelings/opinions regarding the data you have gathered. (Are the results different from what you expected? Did the data validate or alter your focus area? How did the data impact your thinking regarding the focus area?)

The data validated my thoughts yet also went beyond. I had not intended to be able to use the activating thinking strategies as a way to pair students. As I stated, this aspect has been the best outcome. I will continue to find other "good" strategies to include in my lessons.

Position: First-Year Teacher—Art

Interpretation of Research/Data Gathering

Summarize the most significant findings of your research/data gathering as they relate to your focus area. (What important points do the data reveal? What patterns or trends are noted? How do data from various sources compare and contrast? Do any correlations seem important?)

I started out creating a photography curriculum because we do not have one. Now I am focusing only on assessment within the photography curriculum, because if I can come up with an organized system I think it will help students better understand photography. They will know what to look for. I had thought that a final portfolio and notebook was a good idea, but now I see that students need more project beginnings and endings.

Discuss your inferences/feelings/opinions regarding the data you have gathered. (Are the results different from what you expected?

Did the data validate or alter your focus area? How did the data impact your thinking regarding the focus area?)

It is a big help! I guess I need to make a notebook now with each project—with goals, objectives, vocab. listed. I am working on getting goals more completely worked out. I now have a plan for organizing and assessing student work. I will give students a check sheet to put in their notebooks. It will have a place for each assignment, like readings, worksheets, and critiques. Students will self-monitor, and they will know when they are done. I will do a check sheet for each assignment that tells students exactly what they are to do (e.g., color, line, perspective in photo), and I can hand them out before they start working. I will then use the completed check sheet as an assessment.

Interpretation of Research and Data Gathering

Research or data may have been gathered through any number of formats: journals, professional books, online research, interviews, observations, expert sources, classroom experiences and assessments, or any other method the learner chose. The driving focus at this point is for learners to make sense of what has been learned so that it can be applied in their roles. If the project goal needs to be expanded or refined in response to what has been learned, participants should be reminded they have the flexibility to adjust the plan.

Translating New Knowledge Into a Plan

The next section of the learning plan, *translating new knowledge/skills into a plan to meet goals,* prompts reflection on implications of new information for the project goal, identification of actions likely to contribute to goal attainment, and identification of successful outcomes. During this substage, participants also determine how to assess the success of each action they will take to implement learning in their roles, the steps, the time frame to implement each step, and the resources needed to implement the action plan.

Learners at this point in the plan are ready to transfer what they have learned to their roles. While they may or may not reach complete implementation of learning by the close of the staff development program, efforts should be made toward that end. If there are participants who have not gathered enough research or data to complete this section of the learning plan, assure them that it is fine to work at their own pace. They have until the last session to finish.

Individual Work Time and Individual Reflection

The final activities in Session 5 are individual work time and individual reflection. The facilitator should continue responding verbally to individual and group concerns expressed in the journal entries.

Position: Participant A

Translating New Knowledge/Skills Into Plan to Meet Goals

Discuss the implications of your research/data gathering as they relate to your goal and student achievement. (What must you consider as you design a plan for meeting your goal and addressing your responsibilities?)

I must consider time allotment. The activating thinking strategies are important, yet because it is more of a review a large amount of time should not be spent on it daily. It is my responsibility to find and incorporate new, good old strategies into lessons daily.

Identify actions most likely to contribute to goal attainment and improved student achievement. (Focus on one to three strategies, innovations, or changes.)

1. *Write problems that relate to prior lessons yet refer to that day's lesson*

2. *Do the A.T.S. daily*

3. *Make the "levels" of difficulty increase as they are revisited*

For each action listed above, describe how a successful outcome will look.

1. *Correlation between past and new knowledge*

2. *"Starter" every day*

3. *Students being able to perform high level of thinking*

Describe in detail how you will assess the success of each action. Be certain that the assessment and action are compatible, and that both directly relate to your focus area. When appropriate, include copies of any surveys, interview questions, or other assessments. If applicable, provide a description of statistics you will collect, and explain how these can indicate success.

I will write a "starter" on the board daily. Students will work the problems on paper, making notes to self as needed. I will collect the "starters" from them periodically to see what they get or don't get. I will compare that to my observations. I will look at benchmark assessment—meet/did not meet expectations.

For each action, list steps required for implementation and provide a time frame for implementing each step. If the time frame for a step may vary, indicate the criteria that will be utilized to mark conclusion of a step.

1. *Include A.T.S. as "starters" in lesson plans for daily use all year*

2. *Have the "starter" on the board daily—when they enter*

List materials, supplies, or personnel required to implement your action plan.

Other textbooks, workbooks, and teachers for "higher order" thinking skills—for ideas

Position: Special Education Teacher

Translating New Knowledge/Skills Into Plan to Meet Goals

Discuss the implications of your research/data gathering as they relate to your goal and student achievement. (What must you consider as you design a plan for meeting your goal and addressing your responsibilities?)

Since this school uses different achievement assessments than what I am accustomed to giving, I had to learn how to administer the Woodcock Johnson III. After gathering information about the test, I realized I need to

1. *Understand the directions for giving the test so I don't make administration errors*

2. *Become familiar with the materials—protocols, stopwatch, etc.*

As for the implications on student achievement, it is clear. I cannot say with certainty how a student is achieving if I do not give the test correctly.

Identify actions most likely to contribute to goal attainment and improved student achievement. (Focus on one to three strategies, innovations, or changes.)

I have set up observation sessions. I will give the test to a student while being observed by a fellow teacher.

For each action listed above, describe how a successful outcome will look.

I will give the test with confidence, appropriate voice, clear diction, appropriate speed, and without giving verbal or nonverbal hints to students.

Describe in detail how you will assess the success of each action. Be certain that the assessment and action are compatible, and that both directly relate to your focus area. When appropriate, include copies of any surveys, interview questions, or other assessments. If applicable, provide a description of statistics you will collect, and explain how these can indicate success.

A rubric will be developed to assess the administration of the test:
1. Poor   2. Needs Improvement   3. Satisfactory   4. Excellent
Areas to be assessed: confidence of test giver, loudness vs. softness of voice, clarity of diction, speed at which test is given, ease of test taker, lack of response between questions

For each action, list steps required for implementation and provide a time frame for implementing each step. If the time frame for a step may vary, indicate the criteria that will be utilized to mark conclusion of a step.

I hope and plan to be proficient at giving the WJ-III by the end of this semester. After being observed, rated/critiqued, and encouraged, I hope I will be able to administer the test correctly. I will be able to practice several times because I have to give the test to many students due to reevaluations and annual reviews.

(Continued)

(Continued)

List materials, supplies, or personnel required to implement your action plan.

1. *Woodcock Johnson testing booklet*

2. *Protocols*

3. *Pencil*

4. *Stopwatch for fluency section*

5. *Scoring manual*

6. *Scrap paper for math calculations*

7. *Quiet room or setting*

8. *Fellow teacher to observe*

9. *Rubric for teacher to assess administration*

SESSION 6

Session	First 15 Minutes	Next 30 Minutes	Body of Session 90 Minutes	Final 15 Minutes
6	Group Reflection	Mini-lesson: Gathering Alternate Forms of Data in Your Classroom/Role	Individual Work Time	Individual Reflection

By Session 6, learners should be deeply steeped in their projects. This session is devoted to reflection, learning how to gather alternate forms of data, and independent work time.

Group Reflection

Session 6 opens with group reflection and commitment to activities during individual work time. Afterward, the mini-lesson is covered. No new sections of the learning plan are addressed during this session.

Mini-Lesson

The mini-lesson is on alternate forms of data that can be collected in one's role. The purpose of this lesson is help learners think beyond pre- and post-tests as forms of data. As an initial activity, participants are asked to draw diagrams of desks in their particular classrooms. Administrators or other educators could draw a sketch of the school. Everyone is then asked to note on the diagram where most of their time is spent and to analyze the causes for that trend. Further, they are asked to determine how their concentration of time in one area impacts those in other areas. Next, they are asked to represent student traffic patterns and evaluate root causes for the patterns. This portion of the mini-lesson should be completed in about 15 minutes.

After completing these exercises, participants are asked to consider their roles and projects. Each person is then to determine a form of data that could be collected to give information about project success or effectiveness. For example, a pair of vocational teachers researched and began implementing a computerized vocational assessment in their school. As an alternate form of data collection, they designed a student survey to assess "user friendliness" of the program. While participants are not required to collect data, the activity leads them to consider a variety of measures they had not originally considered in the project design and may opt to incorporate.

Individual Work Time and Individual Reflection

The remaining activities during Session 6 are individual work time and individual reflection. Learners should be reminded that only two sessions remain. During the last session, time has not been allotted for individual work as Session 8 is devoted to assessing progress and presenting projects. Session 7 will be the final working session of the program.

SESSION 7

Session	First 15 Minutes	Next 30 Minutes	Body of Session 90 Minutes	Final 15 Minutes
7	Group Reflection	*Learning Plan:* Self-Directed Study (Implementation of Plan to Meet Goals Section)	Individual Work Time	Individual Reflection

This last working session is devoted to reflection, noting how actions taken to implement learning worked, and individual work time.

Group Reflection

Session 7 opens with group reflection and commitment to activities for individual work time. At this time, participants need to assess whether or not goal attainment is possible within the final 90 minutes of work time provided. An appropriate commitment should be made: Complete the project as planned during remaining work time, revise the goal, or work at home before the next session.

Learning Plan: Self-Directed Study

Participants now consider how the actions they took to implement their learning fared through completion of the next part of the learning plan, *implementation of plan to meet goals.* The reflective prompts here lead learners to consider how well the specific actions they took to implement learning worked.

Reflections on Actions Taken to Implement Learning

In this stage, results of actions taken to implement learning are listed along with the participant's opinions regarding the action plan. The purpose of this section is to prompt reflection on the process used to accomplish the project goal. Specifically, the learner is to assess how the process he or she used to implement learning in his or her role impacted progress toward the goal.

Position: Participant A

Implementation of Plan to Meet Goals

List the actions taken and their accompanying steps. For each step, note comments, results, or other pertinent information relating to the implementation of your action plan. Include any deviations from the plan and reasons for the change.

I started focusing on the starter as an A.T.S. This made me spend more time developing my daily starters. I made sure that the starters were increasing in level-thinking and related to topics they learned or used in the course. I found that some days I needed to focus on topics they should have mastered in the past but could not recall with ease.

List your response/opinion/feelings regarding the action plan(s). Did the process occur as you had envisioned it? Why or why not? What information did you gain? Are there steps you would eliminate, add, or alter?

Overall the use of Activating Thinking Strategies has been informative for both myself and my students. The process has progressed as I envisioned because I realized that it would involve planning time and the recall would be beneficial to students. Students' ability to recall previous topics and apply that knowledge has increased. I see it on tests.

**Position: Veteran Teacher—New
to Special Education, Training in Progress**

Implementation of Plan to Meet Goals

List the actions taken and their accompanying steps. For each step, note comments, results, or other pertinent information relating to the implementation of your action plan. Include any deviations from the plan and reasons for the change.

I took an inventory of the tests that were available at the school for special education teachers to use to evaluate students. I then read through each manual and made an outline of the information in the manual. Outlines were completed for 6 different tests. After outlines were completed, I typed them up and compiled a manual. I then studied the instructions for administering and scoring one achievement test and one behavioral inventory. I practiced giving the tests and scoring them. I had to have help scoring the behavioral test. I practiced giving the tests until I could give them and score them on my own.

List your response/opinion/feelings regarding the action plan(s). Did the process occur as you had envisioned it? Why or why not? What information did you gain? Are there steps you would eliminate, add, or alter?

I feel like the action plan worked well. The process occurred just as I had envisioned that it would. I went step by step, and the data was easy to find. I gained information about what tests were available and how to administer them. I would not eliminate, add, or alter the steps. They worked well as they were.

Individual Work Time and Individual Reflection

The remainder of Session 7 is devoted to individual work time and individual reflection. Participants should complete projects either in this session or before returning for Session 8. The last session will be spent finishing the learning plan and giving presentations on projects.

Expectations for Presentations During Final Session

Note that the thought of presenting projects to the group can produce anxiety for some individuals. As with the whole project, learners have control over the type of presentation they will make. Presentations can be informal discussions, or they can involve a prepared speech with visuals and handouts. It is likely that a range of presentations will be presented. Regardless of the format, each learner should be prepared to tell the following: original project goal, summary of research/data gathering, how learning was transferred into an action plan, progress made toward goal, and further learning that could be pursued with the project. This is a time of celebration, and participants should share with the group in a manner that is comfortable and also represents their achievement.

SESSION 8

Session	First 15 Minutes	Next 30 Minutes	Body of Session 90 Minutes	Final 15 Minutes
8	Group Reflection	*Learning Plan:* Self-Directed Study (Post-Project Assessment, Summary/ Interpretation of Post-Project Assessment Sections)	Presentations	Individual Reflection

Session 8 concludes the standard professional development program. Its activities include reflections, presentations, and completion of the final pages of the learning plan.

Group Reflection and Presentation Preparation

This last session opens with group reflection and an opportunity to prepare for presentations. Reflections on this day seem to carry a tone of relief that projects are concluded. As well, individuals appear pleased with their accomplishments in such a brief amount of time. For those who did not meet the goals they originally established, a feeling of failure may present. It is important that the facilitator lead these individuals to assess the progress they did make and encourage them to continue work on the projects until they are completed.

Learning Plan: Self-Directed Study

After group reflection, the final portion of the learning plan is to be completed. The third phase of "self-directed learning" includes *post-project assessment* and *summary/interpretation of post-project assessment*.

Post-Project Assessment to Evaluate Participants' Learning

Post-project assessment includes summarizing the type of post-assessment used, noting whether it was that originally intended or a different assessment, and describing the results. This is the final measurement of the degree to which the participant grew in knowledge base or skill. Clear data relating changes should be described.

Summary/Interpretation of Post-Project Assessment and Assessment of Related Student Achievement

In concluding the final substage, *summary/interpretation of post-project assessment* draws the project to a close through reflection on results of the post-project assessment, description of progress in relation to indicators of success, discussion of implications, identification of new growth or interest areas, summarization of the impact of development in the focus area on ability to carry out professional responsibilities, and noting how student achievement was impacted.

In this final section, distinct data should be listed, clearly defining how participant learning and related actions affected student achievement. The methods of assessing student achievement identified in early planning may be used or additional measures may be included. Regardless of the data used, the direct impact of participant learning on student achievement should be described. In this situation, annual standardized assessments are likely inadequate to measure the impact of a single intervention within a specified number of weeks or months. If no impact on student achievement was noted, or a decline occurred, participants should speculate as to why when responding to the final learning plan prompt. If factors other than the teacher's intervention may have contributed to increases in student achievement, those should be described as well.

Position: Participant A

Post-Project Assessment

Discuss the design of your post-project assessment. Did you utilize the method you originally planned? If not, why did you select a different measure, and how does it compare to the pre-project assessment you conducted?

I used what I planned. I compared the number of A.T.S. used prior to this plan to the number I now use. I also saw improvement in student achievement on the benchmark tests and regular tests.

Describe the results of your post-project assessment, focusing on outcomes you had hoped to achieve and indicators of success identified at the onset of your project.

For me, I have started using A.T.S. as starters daily and sometimes at the end of class to stress different points. I hoped my test scores would improve and they have by a good 10 plus points on average. The C students now maintain B's. Students have also responded that the starters helped maintain their knowledge.

Summary/Interpretation of Post-Project Assessment

Based upon the results of post-study assessment of your growth, did you encounter the outcomes you hoped to achieve as a result of study in the focus area? Explain.

(Continued)

(Continued)

The outcomes were as I expected. Student achievement was impacted because their test scores have improved on average 10 points and they have quicker recall of prior knowledge. You know what you use, you forget what you don't. So, we use the knowledge we learned in the past.

Describe progress in relation to indicators of success identified at the onset of the study. What degree of progress was made in relation to these indicators? After concluding your development in the focus area, do you feel the indicators identified are appropriate measures of success?

In previous years I would use the "starter" idea when I knew my lesson would not take the entire period to cover. I also never really paid attention to what the starter A.T.S. was about. Now I use starters every day, sometimes twice. I feel that the A.T.S. level and number of A.T.S.'s used do measure a success for my plan.

Discuss the implications of your results.

I spend less time reviewing topics before tests and or lessons. I can now spend time getting students to that higher level of thinking—drawing their own conclusions and making their own connections. Because of these things I can spend much more time on new material.

As a result of your development in the focus area, what further interest areas, questions, or growth opportunities have you identified?

I want to begin to make some more interactive openers on the computer. I will refine my A.T.S. to achieve more higher-level thinking.

Summarize the impact of development in the focus area on your ability to carry out your responsibilities. Discuss how student achievement was impacted. Describe results of collected data.

This process has helped me teach. I no longer have to spend part of "lesson" time on content they should already know. I get to spend more time on developing new or extended knowledge.

Results of data show a steady increase in most students' test grades. A.T.S. did this—it was the only change I made. Also, the benchmark tests showed the best reason for using A.T.S.—my class scored the best overall in all the algebra classes at the school!

6 Average Students' Test Grades Across Term

S1: 40, 80, 85, 88, 90, 91   *S4: 64, 77, 76, 87, 83, 78*

S2: 74, 77, 77, 79, 88, 76   *S5: 52, 92, 79, 85, 89, 92*

S3: 71, 82, 71, 78, 78, 87   *S6: 73, 92, 94, 96, 92, 97*

Position: Reading Teacher

Post-Project Assessment

Discuss the design of your post-project assessment. Did you utilize the method you originally planned? If not, why did you select a different measure, and how does it compare to the pre-project assessment you conducted?

The post-assessment was to measure how well I had learned to use a spreadsheet program to show reading progress of students. Yes, I was able to use the measure I selected.

Describe the results of your post-project assessment, focusing on outcomes you had hoped to achieve and indicators of success identified at the onset of your project.

I did learn how to use the spreadsheet, so the results of the post-project assessment were what I anticipated. In analyzing student performance with the spreadsheet, I discovered students achieved at a higher level than I originally thought.

Summary/Interpretation of Post-Project Assessment

Based upon the results of post-study assessment of your growth, did you encounter the outcomes you hoped to achieve as a result of study in the focus area? Explain.

Yes. I met my goal of being able to use the spreadsheet to track student progress.

Describe progress in relation to indicators of success identified at the onset of the study. What degree of progress was made in relation to these indicators? After concluding your development in the focus area, do you feel the indicators identified are appropriate measures of success?

The indicator of success I listed was that I could present the skills learned to the group and show them examples. I can do this. I can also use the spreadsheet to show that my students progressed at a rate faster than I had anticipated.

Discuss the implications of your results.

I learned the reading program I am using works when it is taught correctly.

As a result of your development in the focus area, what further interest areas, questions, or growth opportunities have you identified?

I plan to continue to improve. I want to be able to interpret the scores obtained in order to better understand the deficit areas and to interpret progress made by students. I do not have any further interest concerning the spreadsheet.

Summarize the impact of development in the focus area on your ability to carry out your responsibilities. Discuss how student achievement was impacted. Describe results of collected data.

By learning how to track student performance on the spreadsheet, I now know what success can be generated using the reading program I am using. The spreadsheet did not impact student achievement, but it let me know what I was doing with the reading program was effective in improving student achievement.

Presenting Projects

After completing this final portion of the learning plan, group members present their projects. The facilitator should make a point to offer constructive feedback to each participant, recognizing the effort and hard work that was applied in completing the project. Other group members should be given an opportunity to ask questions and make comments, as they have been critical supports in the process. This time is ultimately to be a positive reflection of professional growth and achievement.

Individual Reflection and
Request for Program Feedback

The final activity of the session is the individual reflection. This is an opportune time for the facilitator to request feedback on the program design and implementation. If a trusting relationship has been established, learners will provide honest feedback that will be useful in refining the program. This last journal entry, as well, provides learners the chance to bring closure to the experience. They should be encouraged to write any response they see fit to compose.

CONCLUSION

"Self-directed learning" comprises the majority of the staff development program, and it is the most lengthy portion of the learning plan. By consistently guiding learners through each phase of the plan, and supporting them in development of self-directedness, the facilitator can nurture a successful experience. Throughout this phase of learning, it is critical the facilitator remind individuals they are in control of their learning and support them in the learning process.

Self-directed learning is conducted in Sessions 2 through 8. During this time, participants can be expected to refine project goals or plans in response to learning. This is a natural part of the process. Learners should be encouraged to adjust plans in response to learning and timelines, so that projects can be completed by the close of the staff development program. It is better to find success with a small goal than to leave the program falling short of a large goal.

8

Incorporating Learning Plans Into Existing Professional Development Programs

With federal and state legislation driving student achievement and professional development, many districts have adopted broad scale improvement models, such as Max Thompson's Learning Focused Schools, Total Quality Management, or the Brazosport model. Use of a packaged reform model does not preclude use of individualization. As a matter of fact, self-directed learning helps teachers develop proficiency with practices embedded in other models by providing choice and direction to improve their performance.

CASE STUDY

To demonstrate, consider the reform measures at one high school. As part of a schoolwide improvement plan and in response to failure to meet adequate yearly progress (AYP), the school adopted Max Thompson's Learning Focused Schools model. Inherent in the model is curriculum alignment; creation of benchmark assessments; long-term and short-term planning by teachers; incorporation of best practices in lesson instruction and assessment; and teacher, school, and district level data analysis for instructional planning. The model is comprehensive, and teachers were included in all aspects of the model. As well, they were required to attend weekly training sessions to learn and practice strategies incorporated in the model. It goes without saying, teachers were overwhelmed and somewhat hostile to the intrusion of yet another "program."

In addition, timing would have it that state accountability measures required documentation; each teacher set and pursued both professional development and student achievement goals. Within the first two and a half months of school, rumors were rampant that large numbers of teachers would not be returning the next year. Despite the staff's willingness to do what was in the best interest of students, demands of the multiple initiatives spurred anxiety, fear, and disdain.

In an attempt to streamline requirements of the schoolwide improvement model and state mandates, the learning plan was used as a linking component. While teachers did not go through 20 hours of staff development to complete a project, they identified professional improvement goals and student achievement goals that were directly connected to reform model strategies. Simply put, teachers identified one or two strategies from the Learning Focused Schools model in which they would become proficient by the close of the school year. The following examples were typical.

Teachers completed components of the plan during the weekly staff development sessions. They set goals linked to student achievement, identified pre- and post-assessment measures, and created a plan for developing knowledge and skill. They progressed through the individualized development process while immersed in the larger professional development program. Anxiety was reduced when teachers realized they were not expected to immediately become experts in all facets of the reform model. They could focus their efforts on manageable pieces of the model in a way that would allow them to feel capable and successful.

A further benefit of merging the learning plan into the reform model was support given through training sessions. The reform model inherently addressed assessment at multiple levels, so teachers received the guidance they needed to appropriately set and measure goals and their impact on student achievement. They were not left to their own devices to comprehend and meet state requirements. By funneling all requirements through the learning plan, which was to be completed over the course of a school year, somewhat of a "release valve" was provided for the mounting pressure teachers felt.

Position: High School Science Teacher

IDENTIFYING FOCUS

Area of interest or targeted change/improvement:
Lecture strategies

Describe how development in this area will improve student achievement. Include background data regarding this area. Describe desired student achievement outcomes that can be verified with data.

Students will have a more positive response to lectures, higher comprehension, and lectures will suit different learning styles. About 30% of students say they like lectures. Test scores average in the 70s. The desired outcome is average test scores in the 80s at a minimum.

How does this relate to school and system goals?

This is part of the Learning Focused Schools strategies for our system and school.

Position: Health Occupations Teacher

IDENTIFYING FOCUS

Area of interest or targeted change/improvement:
Student summarizing strategies

Describe how development in this area will improve student achievement. Include background data regarding this area. Describe desired student achievement outcomes that can be verified with data.

It will help students pull together what they learned during the class. They will store the information and we will use it to start the next class and review over the semester. If students can summarize for each class, it builds until they can summarize an entire unit. Students can also go on to use what they learned in my class about summarizing in other classes. I have never used summarizing, so I don't have any background data. I hope test scores and lab grades improve. I will compare grades before summarizing was used to grades after.

How does this relate to school and system goals?

It is part of the LFS plan to improve achievement.

Position: Learning Focused Schools Teacher Leader

DEFINING THE PROGRAM

List the goals you hope to accomplish as a result of developing your knowledge and skills in the focus area. Phrase the outcomes as observable behaviors.

- *Use rubrics in assessment*
- *Use effective summarizing strategies*

Identify the process(es) you will use to assess *your* pre- and post-project levels of performance, behavior, thinking, understanding, etc. Be certain these assessments correlate with the outcomes you hope to achieve as a result of study in the focus area.

- *Increased use of rubrics*
- *Rise in post-test scores on unit tests*
- *Improvement in student content-related writing as shown on rubrics*

Identify indicators of success that demonstrate achievement of study goals.

- *Students will be engaged and interested*
- *They will show mastery of content*
- *I will be observed implementing the strategies*

Identify the methods you will use to demonstrate the impact your study will have on student achievement. What data will you collect to measure change?

- *Change in average test scores after summarizing strategies are implemented*
- *Improvement in content-related writing based on rubric scores as more rubrics are used for assessment*

HOW DO I INCORPORATE THE LEARNING PLAN INTO MY REFORM MODEL?

There are two things to consider when incorporating the learning plan into your organization's reform model. First, how can you use the plan to focus teachers on the reform model's initiatives? Second, how can you support individualized improvement within the larger professional development program? Both of these items will be addressed in this section. A list of possible pitfalls will follow.

Using the Plan to Focus Teachers

The basic learning plan can be used as is, or an adapted version can be created to include prompts specific to the school's reform model. Any changes to the learning plan would likely take place on the first page, the page where duties and responsibilities are listed. By focusing participants on specific responsibilities, the range of possible goals narrows drastically since learning goals are to be clearly derived from responsibilities. The samples included below demonstrate how the "Responsibilities" section of the learning plan can be adapted.

Original Learning Plan

Position: 6th-Grade Language Arts

RESPONSIBILITIES

Organizational Goals

School
Increase reading and math scores on the spring standardized test

District
To become a world-class school system by providing quality instruction, increasing student achievement, and making sure students are prepared for college or work

Instruction
Reading/literature, writing, speaking/persuasive speech, behavior modification, responsibility and respect, technology incorporation, love of reading—increase reading scores on state test as part of school goal

Administration
Student Support Team meetings, parent conferences, team meetings, grade level meetings

Management/Discipline
Hall duty, lunch duty, detention, classroom management and discipline, grades

Other
Beta Club sponsor, vertical team member

In the original learning plan, the "Responsibilities" section includes broad prompts. The purpose for this is to address a broad audience for whom the spectrum of choices is wide open. In the sample titled Learning Focused Schools Model, notice how this section of the plan is modified to prompt for responsibilities related to the Learning Focused Schools reform model.

The next sample shows how the plan could be adapted to address a whole-school initiative to improve writing in the content areas.

Learning Focused Schools Model

Position: Instructional Coach—High School

RESPONSIBILITIES

Long-Term Planning

Since we are on the block schedule, I have to guide teachers in developing semester-long instructional plans. The plans should include units to be taught, sequencing, pacing, and importance of each unit (essential, important, or compact). Plans should be adjusted across the semester in response to needs of students.

Short-Term Planning

I have to guide teachers in development of unit plans and lesson plans. The unit plan lists what teachers want students to know by the end of the unit. It includes the unit essential questions, major concepts, steps to implement the unit, and assessment strategies. Plans for each lesson should be included with the unit plan. Lesson plans should give the essential questions, tell how students will be initially engaged in the lesson (draw on prior knowledge, vocabulary activity, interest builder), how the content will be delivered in a way that engages students, summarizing activity, extending and refining activity, and assessment method.

Instructional Strategies

During training sessions each week, I will show teachers different LFS strategies they can use to increase student achievement. This is how I will support development of unit plans and lesson plans.

Assessment

As part of the unit and lesson plan, I will show teachers different ways to assess student learning in the classroom. I will focus on using multiple strategies, especially those that show use of information in performance or mastery scenarios or mimic standardized tests.

Data Analysis

I will show teachers how to use various forms of national, state, and local assessments for instructional planning. We will work with individual student data, group data, and whole school data.

Other

I have to guide teachers in developing remedial programs and standardized test review sessions using the LFS concepts.

Writing in the Content Areas
Position: 7th-Grade Math Teacher

RESPONSIBILITIES

Content-Related Writing

- *Give and grade one writing assignment related to math each week*
- *Has to be something using paragraphs*
- *Can do essays, reports, projects, journals, etc.*

Frequency of Writing

- *Show evidence I graded one writing assignment each week*
- *I will use math journals 2–3 times a week—students will explain math processes*
- *Every 2–3 weeks I will assign an essay, report, or project about a math topic*

Assessment

- *Have to use a rubric*
- *Most credit has to be given for content*
- *Require: complete sentences, full paragraphs, correct English*

Team Collaboration

- *Work with English teacher on rubric*
- *Integrate topics from other classes when they fit*

The adaptability of the "Responsibilities" section provides an easy avenue for focusing teachers. Since they are to design the learning plan around their interests and responsibilities, this page can be crafted to zoom in on specific areas of an improvement model or even specific tasks within a more narrowly focused initiative. Notice, though, that the prompt for "Organizational Goals" was removed from the adapted pages. The prompt is unnecessary when all other prompts focus on responsibilities directly connected to the reform model.

Supporting Individualized Improvement Within the Larger Program

Supporting individualized improvement within the larger professional development program relies on use of the learning plan. That alone, though, will not ensure success of individualized learning. A carefully crafted *support plan* should be created *in advance* of incorporating the plan into another program. Four items should be accounted for in supporting individualization:

1. Teacher familiarity with basic components of the reform model

2. Range of choices to be provided in developing goals

3. Inclusion of training in data analysis

4. Regularly scheduled time for work on learning plans

If all four of these items are not addressed, confusion and anxiety can quickly escalate. Imagine this dreary scenario. Teachers have been told that they must improve student achievement scores or all could be in danger of losing their jobs. To their frustration, they will be expected to attend either weekly or bi-monthly training on the new reform model that has been selected for the school. In addition, they must set, pursue, and measure personal goals for improvement and student achievement. And now they have to fill out paperwork for a learning plan on their own, during a planning period that is rapidly disappearing. Chances are, without support, teachers will melt down, mutiny, or simply "make up" information to comply with mandates. In any event, what was intended as a support will be rendered ineffective.

Teacher Familiarity With Basic Components of the Reform Model

Teacher familiarity with basic components of the reform model must occur before the learning plan is introduced. In order to reasonably select a growth area from a range of choices, teachers must understand at a basic level what each choice represents. For example, if teachers know the school reform model focuses on improvement of reading, writing, and math achievement, but have no initial exposure to strategies to be utilized, they cannot adequately select a professional improvement goal that aligns with school improvement initiatives. Similarly, if teachers are told to select among items such as activating strategies, higher-level thinking, differentiation, and performance assessment for improvement goals, but they have no foundational understanding of what these are, they will merely make a random choice instead of an educated decision about improvement.

Based upon my own experience, I suggest that teachers participate in at least three or four information sessions on the reform model before introducing the learning plan. During those sessions, they should become familiar with

- How the overall model works and the purpose for its selection
- Components of the model and their purposes
- Components of the model for which they will be responsible and a clear description of what each component is

If, after these initial information sessions, you find that teachers still have difficulty understanding the model, and therefore will have difficulty setting goals, wait until the group understands the reform model before continuing with the learning plan. I learned the hard way that premature introduction of the learning plan quickly incites anxiety. As well, it later creates extra work for participants, as they come to understand expectations and have to rewrite goals and plans. If you realize you have introduced the plan too early, it is best to collect the packets and explain that you would like to do a better job preparing the group before continuing.

I found that with regular, high-quality, job-embedded staff development sessions, teachers came to understand the overall reform model fairly quickly. After providing opportunities for them to practice a few of the model's strategies and plan for their use in the classroom, they had the foundational experience to plan for their own growth. At this point, the group as a whole is ready to work on the learning plan.

Range of Choices to Be Provided in Developing Goals

Next, the range of choices to be provided in developing goals is drawn directly from the reform model. Will individuals be allowed to direct their goals toward any component of the reform model, or will they be asked to focus on only a few of the components? Here it is important to consider both the school's overall goals and the teachers' developmental needs. If the school's immediate goal is to improve scores on standardized tests of reading and math, but the purpose of the reform model is to change overall instructional practice, is it more beneficial to focus all goals on reading and math or to allow any goal based on model-related strategies? As well, if an individual is a master teacher of reading whose group scores are consistently high, will she be directed to develop a reading goal simply because that is the school initiative, or will she be allowed to write a goal in what is truly a growth area associated with the new model?

The range of choices to be provided should always be dependent upon school goals derived from student achievement data. The needs of a high school, which employs content area experts, will be different from an elementary school where development of basic reading, writing, and math skills is paramount in almost all teachers' roles. It is assumed the reform model was selected in order to meet school goals as well, but it could have purposes larger than a single goal or two. Therefore, careful thought should be given when determining the range of choices for goal selection. Goal attainment will involve a substantial amount of time, and it should be time well spent for the teacher, students, and the school.

Inclusion of Training in Data Analysis

Inclusion of training in data analysis is essential when asking participants to set and meet goals. My experience has been that a fair number of teachers need assistance in measuring their knowledge or skill level before and after completion of projects. The identification of a goal is generally much easier for them than determining how to measure their growth. Further, with reform models inherently focused on improved student achievement, it is important for teachers to understand how data reflect not only their own growth but that of their students.

In order to effectively understand how to analyze and interpret data, both for goal setting and growth measurement, teachers should develop a foundational understanding of at least the following:

- Terminology associated with qualitative and quantitative data analysis (see Chapter 7)
- Local, state, and national standardized tests—both criterion based and norm referenced
- Types of standardized test scores—standard, age related, and so on
- A wide variety of classroom assessments—tests, rubrics, authentic activities, performance-based activities, and so on (see Chapter 7)
- Non-traditional data collection methods—how to devise them to show patterns and growth (see Chapter 7)

It is best to provide participants with an overview of the data they should understand and have them practice reading and interpreting those data to make instructional decisions. Two items are included that can be used for these purposes. Figure 8.1 provides an overview of standardized test data. Figure 8.2 is a sample worksheet for comparing different types of standardized scores. After the group has developed a working understanding of data analysis, they are better able to identify methods for measuring their own growth and student achievement.

A number of factors will impact the level of data analysis proficiency teachers bring with them: teacher preparation programs, professional development, school and district activities, and previous experience with data analysis. It should not be assumed that most teachers understand data and know how to use them. In some cases, only a relatively minor amount of training is necessary to polish teacher skill. In other cases, though, due to a lack of understanding, some teachers and their students have appeared to erroneously "lose" progress simply because the teacher did not know how to select and represent pre- and post-intervention data. Any time spent ensuring teachers understand how to read and utilize data cannot be poorly spent.

Regularly Scheduled Time for Work on Learning Plans

Regularly scheduled time for work on learning plans serves a couple of purposes. First, teachers are provided a specific time to work on their goals and receive help doing so. Second, the facilitator can determine how individuals are progressing, who needs help, and what group direction should be given. Sessions may be brief, such as 10 to 15 minutes during a regularly scheduled staff development session, or they may be longer and focused only on learning plan activities. Whatever the case, time to work on the plan should be provided on a routine basis and in the presence of the learning plan facilitator, who can provide support.

Within the larger reform model staff development program, teachers may only need 10 to 15 minutes a couple of times a month to work on the

Overview of Standardized Test Data

TERMINOLOGY

Ability Test: Ability tests give an indication of a child's general ability. IQ tests are one form of ability test. Typical ability tests administered in schools to large groups of students are the Cognitive Abilities Test (CogAT) and the Otis Lennon School Abilities Test (OLSAT). The scores are most often reported according to standard scores (mean = 100, standard deviation = 15). Local schools may obtain parental permission to administer individual ability tests such as the Kaufman Brief Intelligence Test (KBIT).

Achievement Test: Achievement tests give an indication of a child's performance. Typical achievement tests are the Iowa Test of Basic Skills (ITBS) and the Stanford 9. Scores are generally reported in percentiles (mean = 50, highest score = 100). These scores are often reported to the media and used to compare schools. *Note: Achievement test scores are highly correlated to socioeconomic status and educational level of the mother.*

Norm-Referenced Test: The results from norm-referenced tests provide an indicator of how the student compared to other students, although not necessarily other students taking the test at the same time. Usually the scores are presented in percentiles or grade equivalents. Examples of norm-referenced tests include the SAT, ACT, CogAT, OLSAT, ITBS and Stanford 9.

Criterion-Referenced Test: The results from criterion-referenced tests indicate specific, predetermined knowledge and skills demonstrated by the student. Examples include high school exit exams, such as the California High School Exit Exam and the New York State High School Regents Examinations, and other tests of content knowledge like the Connecticut Academic Performance Test, Alabama Direct Writing Assessment, and the Georgia Criterion-Referenced Competency Tests. Results generally describe a degree of mastery, such as "did not meet expectation," "meets expectation," and "exceeded expectation."

GENERAL ACHIEVEMENT PATTERNS

A–B Students: 80th and 90th percentile ranges on achievement tests

B–C Students: 60th and 70th percentile ranges on achievement tests

C–D Students: 50th percentile range on achievement tests

D–F Students: Below 50th percentile on achievement tests

Note: Although the 50th percentile is the mean, students performing at this level generally do not find school tasks easy. It is important to keep in mind that standardized tests were normed on thousands of children, and students are compared to that norming sample, not to all children who took the test at the same time.

COMPARING ABILITY SCORES TO ACHIEVEMENT SCORES

Be certain to compare scores using the same scale, such as percentiles or standard scores. By using the Data Interpretation Worksheet, scores do not have to be converted. When scores have been plotted, notice in which areas ability and achievement are similar and different. Consider the following rules of thumb:

- A disparity in ability and achievement scores may indicate learning difficulties. Do not discount, though, that perhaps a student did not give his or her best performance.
- An individual student's strengths and weaknesses can vary widely. Test scores may provide some insight into class performance. A disparity of 20 points between scores may be a red flag for a learning disability.
- Students with an ability score in the 90s or below and achievement scores below the 50th percentile can be expected to struggle

Figure 8.1   Overview of Standardized Test Data

TEST DATA INTERPRETATION WORKSHEET

Directions: Using the scale at the top of the page, place a mark on the bottom portion of the worksheet in the place that best represents each student score. By the mark, write the numeric score, what the score represents, and the test name. After all information has been transferred to the worksheet, analyze trends in the data.

SS		70		85		100		115		130
%ile	10	20	30	40	50	60	70	80	90
Stanine		1		3		5		7		9

Significantly Below Average		Average		Above Significantly
	Below Average		Above Average	

Codes:

SS–Standard Score (Mean = 100), %ile–Percentile (Range 1–100, Mean = 50)

Figure 8.2   Test Data Interpretation Worksheet

plan. Under this arrangement, teachers gather knowledge about the reform model concepts during the staff development sessions, receive guidance regarding their learning plan goals, and then independently collect information and pursue goals. The purpose of the plan in this case is to nurture and support the developmental process, not facilitate it entirely during the staff development sessions.

In order to account for individual goal setting, some districts have crafted general templates for documenting goals, data collection, and resulting progress. While these general templates ask the most basic questions included in the learning plan, there is a major difference between these general templates and the learning plan. The learning plan supports the learning process beyond just goal setting and evaluation; it prompts reflection, methodically directs the learning process, and guides individuals toward implementation of learning within their roles.

PITFALLS

There are a few pitfalls that can decrease the effectiveness of the learning plan in supporting individualized development within the reform model. They are as follows:

1. *If the learning plans are not reviewed on a regular basis, teachers forget their goals.* In this case, chances are if the learning project is completed at all, it will be done hastily and lose its potential impact for teacher growth.

2. *If the time frame for completing the project is drawn out too long, teacher proficiency with the reform model concepts may surpass the plan for growth they created.* When this occurs, teachers become confused and do not know

how to complete the learning plan and project. Learning plan activities then appear as busy work and reflective thinking is diminished.

3. *If the facilitator is not present to guide teachers through development and implementation of the learning plan, many will not understand how to work though the individualized learning process.* There is a bell curve in learning independently, and teachers should not be left to figure out the plan on their own. While a few teachers may "get" the process quickly, some individuals would not complete the plan and others would "play the paperwork game" by filling in the blanks without actually completing the project.

4. *If the learning plans are not kept in a central location or by a central person, many teachers lose the materials or do not complete them.* While it is certainly fine for individuals to keep their learning plans, I found management most effective when the plans were distributed and collected during each work session. I provided each teacher with a pocketed folder and stored these folders in a transportable crate. Teachers "checked out" their folders as they needed or wanted them.

CONCLUSION

The learning plan can be used to focus teacher efforts within the context of a larger reform model while still providing for individualization. The plan can be adapted to focus on concepts embedded in the reform model or used in the original format. While employing the learning plan to further teacher development within the reform model, it is important to provide support for individualization. If appropriate support is not provided, several pitfalls could reduce the likelihood of individual success.

9

Adjusting the Model to Meet School and District Needs

Professional learning that is individualized and self-directed can take place in a number of styles and formats. The primary model presented in this book was designed to take advantage of the benefits of self-directed learning and account for deficits of the learning format related in the body of research (Corabi, 1995; Craft-Tripp, 1993; Duron, 1994). Specifically, the model was developed to improve upon previous self-directed models by incorporating support for independent adult learning and embedding an accountability measure to demonstrate growth did occur.

Just as individual learners' needs differ, schools' and districts' needs will differ as well. In response, altering the structure of the professional development program makes logical sense. There are several things to consider, though, in order to make sure the model works and its benefits are maintained.

Factors to Consider in Planning

When, How Often, and Where to Meet

Materials and Their Organization

Selection of an Appropriate Facilitator

Philosophy:
This is a venture to empower adults to develop themselves.

In Chapter 2, factors to consider in structuring the staff development program were discussed. In restructuring the model to meet your group's needs, these same factors should be considered. The next sections, organized by "Factors to Consider in Planning," provide a series of questions to consider when changing the structure of the program to meet your needs. The first few question diagrams will address larger conceptual questions and will show divergent options and what they imply. These "yes-no" questions lead you to consider issues that drive the structural framework of your program. Afterward, logistical questions will be presented. These questions prompt consideration of how often and where sessions will be held, types of materials and organization necessary, and types of facilities needed. Following each question, a brief explanation will expound upon the issue.

WHEN, HOW OFTEN, AND WHERE TO MEET

As noted in Chapter 2, there are two key ideas to remember when structuring meetings:

- Time is a precious commodity
- Meetings must take place in a location, for a duration, and at a time when individuals can settle into solid mental activity

There are a number of formats during which that could occur. The original structure of eight sessions for 2.5 hours after school was selected in order to provide for job-embedded learning (learning that occurs within the context of one's role), provide time for deep learner engagement, and align with state mandates for earning staff development units.

In a later run of the program, 13 sessions of roughly 90 minutes were held during the school day during teachers' planning periods. While this format was not as qualitatively successful as the afterschool sessions, participants did complete their learning projects. And, there were a few lessons for planning learned from that run. First, it was discovered when using this format that, on the whole, the staff development program can operate during the school day. Second, it is absolutely essential the facilitator carefully manage materials and time so learners have real opportunities for deep mental engagement. The first seven of the following questions will help you determine when, how often, and where you should schedule professional development meetings when restructuring the program to meet your needs.

For learning to occur in the context of learners' roles—to be job embedded—sessions should be scheduled during the time those individuals are actively engaged in their roles. For teachers, that would be during the school year. For district-level personnel or those employed year round, it would be the time during which they are most able to practice in context what they are planning to learn.

Question 1
Is it important for learning to occur in the context of the individual's role?

Yes	**No**
Implication: Sessions should be scheduled during the school year.	*Implication:* Sessions can be scheduled during off-times, such as summer break.

Job-embedded learning is important to consider, as learning should be directed to the participants' roles. When learning at the same time one is engaged in a role, opportunity to test out ideas is provided naturally. As well, during the staff development program learners can begin implementing what has been learned. If sessions are conducted during off-times, like summer break, a divide is placed between learning and the first opportunity for implementation.

Question 2
Will the program focus on reform or school initiatives?

Yes	**No**
Implication: Sessions to support self-directed learning must be integrated into the larger reform model professional development program.	*Implication:* A professional development program founded upon the basic self-directed format described in Chapters 4 through 7 can be implemented.

Because of the stress typically associated with new initiatives, it is important to carefully consider how you will restructure the self-directed model to fit your needs. I recommend making a distinct choice about how you will incorporate self-directed learning:

- Self-directed learning will support a larger professional development program, *OR*
- Self-directed learning will be the predominant professional development model, *OR*
- Self-directed learning will be one choice among a variety of selections for professional development

If the exact role this model will have in the organization's overall professional development plan is determined, it will be easier to account for the multitude of teacher needs in advance of implementation.

As discussed in Chapter 8, if you intend to incorporate the self-directed program into a larger reform model, it fits nicely as a method for focusing teachers on "bite-sized" components of the larger program. In this situation, work on learning plans can occur for brief periods of time, such as 15 to 20 minutes, during a session focused largely on reform concepts. During this 15 to 20 minutes, the facilitator should make a concerted effort to conference individually with all participants to ensure they understand their responsibilities in relation to the self-directed learning that will primarily take place outside the professional development sessions. As well, if not addressed in the larger reform model, the facilitator must incorporate mini-lessons on data analysis.

The number, length, and type of professional development sessions to be held across a school year will have a great impact on teacher morale and perceived stress. While it is possible to have an effective, comprehensive program that involves training as often as once a week, these sessions must be perceived as beneficial by participants. Therefore, the collection of sessions should have a clear focus. If that focus is a reform model, to reduce the number of new concepts to be processed at a given time, self-directed learning would be best intertwined as a supporting element as opposed to an additional, concurrent program. If the self-directed model is the sole professional development program or a choice among programs, sessions should be planned in such a fashion that all the components described in Chapters 2 through 7 are addressed during the program.

Question 3	
Will the self-directed model be the only professional development program offered?	
Yes	**No**
Implication: Scheduling can allow learners options for attending sessions at preferred learning times or at times they can work collaboratively with others having the same interest or focus.	*Implication:* Scheduling may not have the same flexibility for choice of session attendance when multiple learning options are available.

If the self-directed model or a reform model incorporating self-directed learning is the primary model implemented, a variety of session schedules could be offered to participants provided a facilitator is available for the sessions. When using both the basic self-directed program and a larger reform model incorporating the learning plan, I have offered teachers a choice of attending during planning or just after the school day ends. Since only one professional development program was offered at the school to the particular groups of teachers involved, there were no scheduling conflicts and the same session was delivered repeatedly throughout a single day or multiple afternoons in a single week.

By providing the option of attending during planning or after school, a larger number of teachers felt their personal needs were met. The after-school option was especially useful to teachers wishing to collaborate on a single project or similar topics since staggered planning periods, or no planning period at all, eliminated the option to do so otherwise. To be certain, collaborative work fast-tracks the camaraderie and affective support listed as benefits of the model by previous participants (see Chapter 10), in addition to providing an instant milieu for professional discourse.

Clearly, it is not necessary to forgo providing teachers a variety of options for staff development in order to provide for flexibility in session attendance. It is simply easier to increase attendance and reduce stress regarding attendance when teachers can choose the optimal time for their own learning without having to sacrifice one or more other obligations. As well, collaboration that cannot be easily achieved without a variety of meeting times has a greater chance of taking place when participants can select a regular, structured time to work together.

Question 4	
Will sessions be scheduled during the regular workday?	
Yes *Implication:* Sessions will be held during the eight-hour workday.	**No** *Implication:* Sessions will be held before or after school, or they may be held during a break.

This is one of the most important questions you will answer. When considering what time of the day to hold sessions, remember what should be accomplished during a session. If incorporating the activities suggested in this book, that includes

1. Development of self-directed skills through mini-lessons

2. Learning plan work

3. Group reflection

4. Individual reflection

5. Independent work

All these activities require heavy-duty mental processing. The time provided must accommodate what is to be accomplished.

When planning during the day, be mindful that a 50-minute or 90-minute planning period does not provide a full 50 or 90 minutes for staff development. By the time teachers dismiss their students, collect their things, go to the restroom, arrive at the meeting location, and repeat these activities before going back to class, at the very least 10 to 15 minutes have been lost. And the degree of stress created by being on a strict schedule impacts time needed to settle mentally into staff development activities.

If, indeed, you choose to hold sessions during the day for 90 minutes or less, it would be wise to consider alternating mini-lessons and learning plan work across sessions, so that maximum time for independent work is provided during each session. Group and individual reflections should occur each session, as these aid learners in cognitive processing. As well, if managed properly, they will not consume large amounts of time.

While teachers are tied to a bell schedule and constant supervision of students, other educators who are not in teaching roles also have busy schedules. When planning during or after the school day, consider both the professional demands placed upon participants and their biological needs. For example, make sure time is provided for movement to the session location, that bathroom breaks are allotted, and that individuals' typical duties, like hall monitoring, are considered. If big events, like parent conference days, are on the school agenda, consider planning the regularly scheduled session at an alternate time so that the stress of that larger activity does not negatively impact learning. Addressing these issues at the planning stage will provide a smoother experience for the facilitator and learners.

Question 5	
Will there be a strict requirement for hours spent with the facilitator to earn credit for the staff development course?	
Yes *Implication:* Only time in actual sessions will count toward earning professional learning credit.	**No** *Implication:* Individual logs may be used to account for actual time spent on the learning project.

In some cases, individuals are given staff development credit only for actual time spent with the instructor. If that is so for your state or district, then this decision is fairly simple. You would next consider how many meeting hours are necessary to conduct the program.

Another format for the staff development program allows for the use of logs to document actual time spent on the project in addition to time spent in sessions. With this option, the staff developer could structure the program according to one of the following formats:

- Participants attend all sessions and keep a log documenting additional time spent on the project outside of sessions
- Participants have the option of attending only key sessions and documenting remaining time spent on the project in a log

When using a more liberal format, it is extremely important to remember that participants will need academic and emotional support. To totally eliminate the requirement for attendance at training sessions is to greatly reduce the success of the model and the participants.

When allowing individuals to attend only key sessions, a couple of factors need to be considered. First, participants should be required to attend at least two meetings in which the learning plan is developed and reviewed, so that progress and understanding can be assured by the facilitator. As well, participants should attend at least two sessions in which data analysis is practiced. These items could be addressed in the same two meetings, but to do so comprehensively would leave little time for independent work. Since the majority of work on the project would be done outside the sessions, lack of work time during these sessions is not a major concern. Finally, all participants should return for a concluding meeting to share their projects and results and complete the final pages of the learning plan.

Question 6

How often will staff development sessions be held?

How often sessions will be held depends specifically upon

- State and local requirements for earning staff development units
- Total number of hours participants should spend with the facilitator by the close of the program
- The time span over which the project should be completed
- Whether sessions take place during the day, after school, or during breaks
- Whether participants will be required to attend all sessions or only key sessions

In considering the answer to this question, keep in mind that learning should occur across time. While one-week breaks in the fall or spring may seem like an ideal time for teacher development, one week is insufficient to develop learning processes associated with this model. Learning and sessions should be spread across at least a couple of months, so that participants have ample time for academic growth and reflective thought, as well as sufficient time to complete a meaningful project. Remember that the philosophy behind the model is to empower adults to develop themselves.

Question 7

Where will staff development sessions be held?

The choice here is largely dependent upon answers given for the previous four questions. Specifically, these factors will impact where sessions can be held:

- If sessions are held during the school year or during breaks
- If sessions will be scheduled during the regular workday
- If participants will do all work during sessions or attend only key informational sessions and work independently outside sessions
- How often sessions will be held

Time and convenience must be carefully considered so that individuals have adequate opportunity to arrive at the sessions and engage in deep thinking. As well, the meeting location itself should be conducive to the tasks that will take place there. These four situational conveniences should be present:

1. Quiet, comfortable, distraction-free atmosphere

2. Adult-sized tables and chairs

3. Ample room for each learner to spread out materials

4. Sufficient technology for research and data management

With the exception of programs in which participants do independent work outside sessions, such as with infusion into a reform model or using the key sessions and log format, the presence of sufficient technology is quite important. Multimedia tools necessary to conduct projects should be available during work time. Basic resources should include online research capability, a word processing program, a spreadsheet program, and a multimedia presentation program.

Summary

The choice of meeting location will set the stage for learner productivity. If there is ample work space and sufficient technology is provided in a quiet, comfortable setting, participants will generally become engaged in their work and remain on task.

MATERIALS AND THEIR ORGANIZATION

Advance preparation of materials goes a long way toward organizing participant learning and efficient session flow. Whether using the materials provided in this book or creating your own, your program has the greatest chance for success when all materials are prepared in advance of the first session. By issuing all materials for all sessions in a bound fashion on the first day of the program, time is saved in later sessions that can be spent on actual learning instead of administrative tasks. The following two questions will help you consider materials you will use in your restructured program.

Question 8
Will you create your own training documents?

Yes	No
Implication: You must first determind the skills and activities to be addressed in each staff development session.	*Implication:* You may use or adapt the reproducible templates found in Resources A, B, and C of this book.

Part of making the model your own is deciding exactly how you would like to present the staff development program to participants. A large part of the facilitator's role is presenting the program in such a way that it makes sense to learners and facilitates their growth. Therefore, the facilitator should be very comfortable with the materials to be used for mini-lessons and self-directed learning. In the Resources section at the back of this book, the following materials are provided for use by facilitators in training: session agendas for the basic eight-session program, the basic learning plan, some mini-lesson materials, and the individual reflection prompt.

For those who choose to modify the resources from this book or create their own, there are several items to consider so that the materials and their organization support the overall program. The following steps provide a guide to methodically planning for materials:

1. Decide the focus of your program: self-directed learning, reform model, or school initiative.

2. Determine the number and length of sessions.

3. Determine the skills and activities to be addressed in each session, focusing on those necessary to develop self-directed learning, and address the program focus.

4. Create a detailed session-by-session agenda for the entire staff development program (see Resource A for an example). Make sure mini-lessons and learning plan activities, and therefore coordinating materials, build upon one another to support learners' growth in regard to self-directed learning and the program focus.

5. Collect or develop resources for each mini-lesson and organize them according to sessions to be delivered. The learning plan should be kept intact and apart from other session materials so that participants do not have to search by session for each successive part of the plan.

6. In advance of the first session, bind the agenda, materials, and learning plan in a format that is easy for participants to use.

There are as many ways to present self-directed learning as there are facilitators who choose to do so. Creating or modifying materials to suit the facilitator's background knowledge and the intended audience is encouraged so long as a continuum of support is provided with clear, organized, well-prepared documents.

Question 9

What materials are necessary to implement the restructured program?

As noted in Question 8, the primary materials needed for a program incorporating self-directed learning are session agendas, materials for mini-lessons, the learning plan, and individual reflection prompts. Depending upon your restructured model, you will likely need several other supporting documents as well, the most important of which are materials explaining the focus of your program and the purpose for participant involvement.

Take, for example, the school mentioned in Chapter 8. The staff development program implemented was centered around a larger reform model, and the learning plan was incorporated to link state requirements for student achievement and staff development goals to the reform model. In order to fully explain to teachers their role in the reform model and its coordinating professional development program, I prepared a diagram that showed how federal and state requirements for student achievement filtered down to the district and school. Further, I created another diagram and a chart showing teachers the expectations of them in relation to the reform model, including how both the school and teachers would be evaluated. I then explained how the learning plan streamlined several expectations of them into a single document that also supported their growth.

On the whole, the better informed participants are about the reason for their involvement in professional development activities, the more cooperative they are. Since individuals have a variety of learning styles, I highly recommend providing a visual representation of any verbal rationale you will provide regarding the purpose for the professional development program and teachers' role in it.

Summary

Materials and their organization underpin learning across several weeks or months. Time spent efficiently organizing materials in advance of the professional development program is time well spent. In addition to the basic materials needed to organize session activities, deliver mini-lessons, and lead participants through self-directed learning and reflection, additional documents often need to be created to explain the rationale behind the program and learners' roles in relation to the larger school and organizational concerns it supports.

SELECTION OF AN APPROPRIATE FACILITATOR

An appropriate facilitator will be the key to success for the restructured program and its participants. In Chapter 2, the characteristics of an appropriate facilitator were addressed in depth, and those ideal characteristics apply to a restructured program as well. But, in addition to these characteristics, a couple of other questions regarding appropriate facilitators should be addressed for program structures that may not concentrate solely on self-directed learning.

Question 10
Will your program be based on a reform model or content-specific initiatives?

Yes	No
Implication: The facilitator should be something of an "expert" regarding the reform model or content-specific initiatives.	*Implication:* If the program is solely focused on self-directed learning, the facilitator is not required to have content-specific expertise.

If your restructured self-directed program is embedded in a reform model or school initiative, and the facilitator of self-directed learning is also the instructor for the larger professional development program, the facilitator will certainly be required to have content knowledge in the area of the reform model or school initiative. A successful trainer with dual positions of content instructor and facilitator of self-directed learning will easily shift between roles. This person will know when and how to deliver instruction on the school initiative while also permitting choice and self-direction. In order to attain credibility with learners, this facilitator should be well trained and supported for this situation, as it will certainly be a challenging one. Participants will face uncertainty with the reform and self-directed learning, and the facilitator has to be able to manage the group in both respects.

If the facilitator of self-directed learning does not have content expertise related to reform or other initiatives and will not be required to develop the expertise, you might consider pairing two individuals together: one instructor for content of the reform model or school initiative and one facilitator for self-directed learning. In this case, the collaborating "content" instructor must understand the philosophy behind self-directed learning and refrain from behaviors that reduce legitimate choice and opportunity for self-directed learning. Even though largely supported by the facilitator in self-directed learning, participants should still be provided the choice and encouragement to develop self-directedness by both trainers.

Question 11	
Do you want to employ a facilitator?	
Yes	**No**
Implication: Participants are supported in the process of becoming self-directed learners.	*Implication:* Participants are left to navigate self-directed learning on their own.

Self-directed learning implies that one is directing his or her own learning. While this is the case, there is a legitimate role for the facilitator as a supporter of learning. Most adults have not pursued formal learning in the self-directed format and consequently require assistance. In fact, past difficulties with self-directed learning in professional development have been due in large part to the distinct lack of support or assistance for learners. I cannot overemphasize the importance of having a competent facilitator to guide participants through the program.

If indeed you choose to forgo employing a facilitator to direct the program, I suggest providing at least some sort of support through an assigned contact person who can answer learner questions. This might be a district professional development coordinator, building administrator, instructional coach, or master teacher trained to provide learning support to adults. This individual should be no less prepared to deal with the emotional and academic needs of learners than an employed facilitator would be. But again, I highly recommend incorporating a facilitator to run regularly scheduled training sessions so that support can be provided in a structured, predictable format. This model was designed for such routine, systematic support of learners.

Summary

A competent facilitator is crucial to the success of your restructured program. In addition to the skills necessary to implement the basic self-directed program, the facilitator must also be familiar with reform and school initiatives if required to provide instruction associated with them. This particular situation could create a good deal of stress for program participants, and the facilitator should be well prepared for and supported for a dual role. Finally, the importance of a facilitator in guiding adults through formal self-directed learning cannot be overstated. This model was designed to account for deficiencies in other self-directed professional development programs, and use of a trained facilitator was specifically incorporated to address learners' need for support.

PHILOSOPHY

The philosophy behind your self-directed program should guide all the decisions you make in restructuring the program. If the larger philosophy behind using this format for learning in a professional setting is not about empowering adults to develop themselves, then you should define exactly why you have chosen this model. What you ask of participants in their learning pursuits and how the facilitator operates within the learning environment are all driven by the philosophy behind your program. Each decision about the program and how it will be implemented should support the philosophy you have adopted. The following two questions will help you consider philosophy in restructuring your program.

Question 12
Is "This is a venture to empower adults to develop themselves" the underlying philosophy of your structure?

Yes	No
Implication: All decisions about the structure of your program should support adults in making choices about and pursuing their independent study.	*Implication:* The purpose for selecting this model should be considered and a philosophy for using this model should be determined before further planning takes place.

If you accept as your philosophy that espoused in this book, then your restructured program should follow the same tenets as the basic staff development program: Provide instruction and support to adults in becoming self-directed learners, utilize a facilitator as opposed to an instructor, encourage independent and informed decision making, encourage reflection, and provide for group learning or support. If your basic premise for selecting this model does not align with that philosophy, you should define your philosophy before planning your professional development program. Each successive component of your program should align with your philosophy.

Without knowing your philosophy, you lose a degree of focus and direction. It is somewhat akin to hopping on public transportation in a large city. You can ride for quite some time without having to select a destination, always moving toward somewhere. Eventually, though, the ride stops and you must disembark. You may have no idea where you are, especially since you had no idea where you were heading at the outset, and you may be unable to communicate where you would like to be. Without a doubt, in this age of mandated accountability, few organizations have the luxury of allotting resources without knowing what to ultimately expect as a return. Philosophy drives direction and focus, and it should be clearly defined before delving into planning.

Question 13

**In what ways will the structure of your
program support your philosophy?**

Every decision you make about the structure of your professional development program will either support or undermine the philosophy you hold. The following items should be considered in relation to your philosophy when planning your program:

- What is the purpose behind using this model for the participants' professional development?
- What is the ultimate outcome of participant learning?
- What is the legitimate role of the instructor or facilitator in delivering the program and supporting participants?
- What types of mini-lessons or program activities are necessary to support learners in arriving at the larger purpose behind the program?
- How is the whole organization impacted by the program and learner activities driven by the philosophy?

Every choice about every component of the program should be derived from your philosophy. Every component should connect in a clear and direct manner to this broader purpose for the program. The philosophy defines why you are doing what you are doing and provides a reference point for decision making as you restructure the program to meet your needs.

Summary

Philosophy sets the ultimate destination for your self-directed program. It frames the "Why?" behind selecting this particular format for learning. Each choice you make about learner expectations, program activities, and the facilitator's role should be drawn directly from the overarching philosophy.

CONCLUSION

The format of the individualized professional development model can readily be restructured to meet the needs of different schools and districts. Most critical to altering the format of the program is addressing factors to consider in planning: when, how often, and where to meet; materials and their organization; selection of an appropriate facilitator; and the philosophy behind the program. In order to maintain the benefits of the model, restructured formats should account for job-embedded learning, time and setting for participants to engage in deep mental thought, and academic and emotional support of learners.

10

Preparing for Participant Responses to Self-Directed Learning

In my research of this model, the most intriguing results have been those relating to learner thoughts and reactions. Across the professional development program, participants have a diverse array of responses. They bring with them a clear expectation that the program will operate in large part like any other training program they have experienced, and adjusting to the difference is a little unsettling. As they come to realize they are in control of their learning, most experience something akin to a roller coaster of emotions. Eventually, by the close of the program, most learners have transitioned to a reflective state, focusing more on intellectual and academic concerns. Finally, they leave with a sense of empowerment, satisfied their needs have been met. And, largely, their concluding thoughts about the program are very positive.

This format for learning can elicit strong emotional responses from participants, thus understanding what to expect and preparing in advance is very important for facilitators. The next sections are organized according to the types of responses typical of participants in the program. Each section includes comments made by learners during the course of the program. A discussion of suggested facilitator behaviors will follow each description of learner responses.

TYPICAL PARTICIPANT RESPONSES

Adjusting to the Format

Teachers' prior learning experiences lead them to believe there is an inherently correct way to proceed in the individualized staff development program. As such, they seek reassurance that they are proceeding appropriately. It is only through repeated facilitator assurances that there are no correct answers that learners relinquish adherence to this conception.

Despite being given the freedom to design and conduct a learning project of their choice in the manner of their choice, almost all participants initially hold on to the conception there is a "right" way to go about learning. They ask permission for minor items, such as the following:

Can I abbreviate instead of writing out the whole title?

Do I have to write in complete sentences?

I want to change something. Is that o.k.?

In addition to minor items, learners want reassurance they are completing their projects correctly.

You know, I understand what is going on, and I understand the purpose and the goal and all that stuff, but I still like verbal reassurance of it. You know, even if you were to say, "If this is what you want to do, then that's right." O.K. I just want to make sure that I'm not getting off on some tangent, going in a completely wrong way, going left when I should be going right, if that makes any sense.

One teacher explained why it is so difficult for learners initially to accept the idea they are in control.

I think it's just for the fact that we've always been in these classes, even in poetry where there is no right or wrong answer. You break down a piece of poetry into what it means to you, but I was still told I was wrong. Well, they told me there's no right or wrong, but then they told me what I did wasn't right or good enough. I guess it is little things like that. You just never really and truly believe that there's no right or wrong.

It is because of the natural resistance to taking full ownership at the onset of the program that the facilitator must carefully respond to learner concerns. Responses to learner hesitancy must be met with continual patience and reiteration that they, as learners, are in full control. Facilitator behavior at the beginning of the program is critical to development of independence on the part of the learners.

As teachers themselves, facilitators may feel inclined to provide individuals with suggestions for projects and direction in learning options. In the initial sessions of the program, this must be kept to a minimum, as learners will inadvertently get the message that there is a specific project and learning format the facilitator wants. While it is fine to share ideas, use questioning strategies, and guide brainstorming, the facilitator should not endorse one option over another outside of noting if the option addresses school and system goals, student achievement, and the individual's role.

> I think you have told me often enough that I am not supposed to worry about right and wrong, so if you say something often enough, if you throw enough mud, some of it is bound to stick.

Learners will eventually come to accept complete ownership for their learning and understand the role of the facilitator.

EMOTIONAL RESPONSES

Participants' emotional responses tend to revolve around their personal assessment of progress toward their goals. Overall, when they perceive they have failed to make progress *according to the expectations they set for themselves,* they feel negatively about themselves and the program. These feelings are most common in the middle series of sessions. As learners begin to experience success, the tide shifts toward a positive outlook. During any particular session, a participant is apt experience both elation and frustration.

This collection of learner comments shows the range of emotions experienced across the program and their direct connection to progress.

> I'm finding out all kinds of things I didn't know. This is exciting! I mean, really, this will be fun!

> Well, [I felt] insecurity, because I didn't even know the path I was on, much less understand the path I was going to, because I am in totally foreign territory as far as the spreadsheet and database is concerned . . . I was concerned, knowing that this is not a graduate credit for an A or a B or a C or a D, but I could fail. I was getting concerned because I never failed at anything and that I would have to make an excuse as to why it didn't get done.

> I was a little overwhelmed by how much work I was going to have to do to totally develop my curriculum based around a community setting. There's no way I could get all that finished in eight weeks.

When we got together a week and a half ago, or whatever it was, you showed me another way. And I saw it instantly, that it would work, then I was totally relieved.

You know, I don't think I have changed. I'm happier because I've got this thing going. That's a change. You know, I had a question or a query or theory that I could do something, and you have shown me that I can. So we were able to take, you know, my hopes and dreams and make it come true. Sometimes you start these things and say, "It was a good idea, but I can't." And see I know I can, so that's a change I am really positive about.

This class continues to be fun, and I have good feelings about the probability of success.

Negative feelings are almost always associated with work on projects. Particularly, these emotions arise when learners experience confusion, lack of understanding, or barriers to progress. Generally, when these feelings are experienced, they appear outwardly as impatience, frustration, and disappointment.

Inherent to learners' perception of progress is their perception of themselves in relation to others. The vast majority of participants compare themselves to others at some time throughout the staff development program. If individuals view themselves as progressing favorably in comparison to others in the group, they feel positively. Conversely, if they view themselves less favorably, they feel less positively.

I don't even know what they are doing. I just hear them talking. I see them working, they're on computers, or they're sitting quietly at a table. I can tell that they're busy doing stuff, and I know that I am busy. I don't know that I'm any farther behind than the next person, but I just feel like I'm behind.

Whether we're supposed to or not, I use the group to see how I'm doing comparatively. You know, all our goals were different, but if people were stuck on something and I'm not stuck on something, and I have a clear mind as to what's going on and other people don't, I'm kind of like, o.k., that's good. Even when I took a defensive driving class, I knew it and they didn't. I was way ahead of them, and if they were going to pass, I know I'm going to.

They were doing things outside the class, but I wasn't. And so I didn't feel I had as much to share as they would when they shared. But towards the end I was doing as much as they were. I feel like toward the end I was. I guess they got a gangbuster start, and I kind of caught up at the end, so I didn't feel quite that bad.

The facilitator should pay close attention to how participants are feeling. If individuals become convinced they will not succeed, their motivation and willingness to continue trying are greatly reduced. They may even avoid attending sessions.

It is crucial that the facilitator inform all learners that they may have ups and downs, and that those ups and downs are common and to be expected. When someone becomes upset, the facilitator best serves that person by trying to uncover the root cause of the problem. I have regularly found questioning—to guide problem identification and solution generation—to be successful in defusing these situations. After determining the problem and selecting a solution, most learners are able to move beyond the barrier. Again, the learner should remain in control of decision making.

After an emotional display, adults often become embarrassed. The facilitator should reassure these individuals that becoming emotional is not necessarily a bad thing. Emotionality is an indication they have taken ownership for their learning and have become intrinsically invested in the task at hand. Monitoring the emotional state of participants is akin to using a barometer to measure their perceptions of their progress. The facilitator would do well to note each group member's typical emotional responses and attempt to head off potentially extreme emotional escalations.

ACADEMIC RESPONSES

Across the staff development program, participants have a variety of responses to their learning. Unlike emotional responses, academic responses are based upon intellectual reflections on learning. Often positive responses are expressed as a result of making progress toward a goal or learning new information. Negative responses to learning often correlate to a lack of progress toward goal completion.

> After intensive searching, I found what I was looking for. I'm on a roll, and I'm feelin' good.

> You take what you can get when you can get it. And with Sally's failure to be able to come through, it wasn't her fault, I mean sick is sick, she was really sick. So, I've never liked cooperative learning. I said that in the beginning, and I still don't like it.

> I do think/hope that this project will be better than I originally anticipated. I am finding out more than I thought I would, and I am pleased with where it is heading.

> I honestly think this project will be productive and successful. Students are more involved than I anticipated, and they are taking it seriously (seeing as it incorporates several grades). I am noting adjustments as I go along, and next year this will be a "killer" unit.

Unlike emotional responses to learning, which are often reactionary, academic responses to learning, even negative ones, are usually based on some degree of analysis or thought about the particular issue. When in disagreement with participants, the facilitator should be careful to "allow" the individuals their opinions. In these situations, facilitators should be mindful of their roles as guides to learners and refrain from debate, even outside staff development sessions, that could initiate a contentious relationship with participants.

Due to the job-embedded nature of the individualized program, many participants naturally process what they are learning in the context of its use in their roles. The following comments by teachers demonstrate the direct tie between learning in the program and professional duties.

> The two girls that just left here, they were working together, even though I'm sitting here. I'm facilitating. It's probably like this staff development. I'm sitting here, I'm listening to them. If I hear something way off target I'm going to lead them back to the right direction, but they're figuring it out together. . . . I think cooperative grouping is great, but when you have 30 kids in a classroom, it's very hard.

> It puts a little thorn in my brain saying keep that in mind. You know people react the quickest to something they don't know. Maybe I can figure out a way, some way to develop in my project, a way to make my guys stimulate, guess their, answer their own problem, figure out things for themselves.

> I already spoke with the students in the classroom [about] what we should change over here and what they prefer to change, or do they prefer to change it. And they're willing to add some more things.

One of the most powerful academic responses from teachers is the translation of learning tenets in the staff development course to practice in the classroom. This occurs naturally, as many teachers come to appreciate the benefits of the model. Most often, forms of individualization, choice, and collaborative work are offered to students.

Purposefully, the design of the learning plan is intended to guide learners to implement actual projects into their roles. When sessions are conducted during the school year or at a time when participants are actively engaged in their professional responsibilities, implementation occurs more quickly. As noted in participant comments, the style and engaging activities of the learning format are also integrated into teacher roles.

By the conclusion of the program, because teachers are in control of their learning, project completion has a powerful impact on their self-esteem. One learner stated, "It's a reflection of me." When final projects are presented at the last session, reports are generally accompanied by a sense of accomplishment and empowerment. The following comments by participants punctuate the point.

> I enjoyed it. I enjoyed it overall, because number one, it was a challenge. I was able to challenge myself to do something, and those are always the kind of, the best rewards, when you challenge yourself to do something, and then you complete it. And you know, like I said, I was proud of my end result, and I was proud of what I accomplished . . . You know, that's kind of a confidence builder.

> It turned out the way that I really wanted, and I feel successful.

> I'm just more comfortable overall. I'm comfortable not worrying about whether I'm doing the right thing, and I'm more comfortable with, with what my project ended up being. Last time we talked, I was still worried about where it was going and what was going to happen and what it was going to end up like. And now I'm actually seeing what it's ending up like, and I like it. I'm more comfortable in my own skin.

Over and over again, these types of comments pour forth from learners. In my role as facilitator, seeing the pride that fellow educators feel as a result of this program similarly excites me and reinforces my drive to bring this experience to them.

THOUGHTS ABOUT THE PROGRAM

Most teachers have never participated in a formal educational situation designed around self-directed learning. Participants quickly recognize the program offers a personal benefit to them, and that benefit often provides the motivation to engage in program activities. Benefits described by learners include the following:

- Opportunity to pursue a goal
- "Forced" completion of a learning activity
- Time provided to work
- Learning based upon individual interest
- Structure of the learning plan organized learning
- Could work independently
- Group setting provided for camaraderie and support

Further, participants reported they are pleased to be in control of their learning experiences. Learners indicate that content learned is specific to their needs and will transfer to their professional roles better than that of other staff development programs. Succinctly stated, the individualized program provides teachers the opportunity to cater learning to their self-assessed needs.

The following comments characterize typical learner conceptions of the self-directed professional development program:

> We're used to going to staff developments where we go in, we sit down, we listen, they speak, we shut up, we get up, we leave, we've got our staff development in the end. We don't have to do anything other than we're supposed to be listening, and you know as well as I know that many times we go to staff developments and we don't listen. We don't, we don't really participate, and that is not what staff development is supposed to be about, because we are certainly not growing professionally. I didn't learn anything from those because I didn't have a vested interest in anything that they were talking about.

> You were actually telling people, "Please, do what you feel is right," and you were giving them the freedom to explore without parameters, because you're not going to know where you're going unless you have no boundaries. I mean, if you put boundaries, then you put limits, and you couldn't find the correct answer. But you were very clear about saying, "Hey, listen, everything is o.k. You just proceed where your guts are taking you." You got sick of saying it, and that was really cool, because we've never done that. I mean in my education you always had limits, and you were saying, "No, be free." And we also know that the whole purpose of this is to have people learn what they want, to do own their own, in their own direction."

> Self-directed learning is enjoyable for me. I don't have to wait on others, my quality of work is more-often-than-not at a higher level, and I can ask questions at my leisure. I'm going to get out of this what I put into it.

> This program has kind of taken all the stuff that I like and wrapped it into one.

In addition to the learning format and the freedom it provides, participants regularly describe support from peers during the process as beneficial. Developing rapport among learners early on is done just for this reason. While there are exceptions, group members' perceptions of one another are generally positive and connote professional respect. The following types of responses are common:

> We've all had a good relationship, so we felt free to talk, speak openly.

Sometimes we got off course, you know, and stuff like that, but there was good camaraderie with the group, I thought.

I just watched Dane handle people that I could not handle, without going crazy, and he does it with such skill and precision and confidence. And I'm just amazed at what he does. And Lily, I've worked with the products of her efforts for as long as I've been here, and I just like the pride she has in her culture and what she is, and how she tries to take her pride and pass it on to her students. They're just two remarkable teachers, and just being with them and sharing, I admire, I get something from it. I admire what they're doing.

I really like this group because we were able to share ideas. Everyone is anxious for the others to be successful in this program. Therefore they are always willing to help.

Even though some participants were initially uncomfortable sharing aloud with the group, it eventually came to be a favored activity for most people. Individuals came to view their peers as almost a support group for learning. The interaction, sharing, and camaraderie led learners to feel safe in the group and in taking risks in learning.

While participants' perceptions of the program are overwhelmingly positive, there are a few predictable areas of discontent. One of those areas concerns the learning plan. Some individuals are frustrated by the open-ended questions, assuming there is a correct answer.

To be perfectly honest, it drove me crazy because I wasn't quite sure what was supposed to go in there. It was so open-ended. I wasn't sure what I was supposed to be doing with it and that, that was frustrating.

I mean I understood it. I don't want to say I didn't know the words or something like that, but I just wanted to make sure that I was going to answer the question you were asking and I didn't have some misconceived notion of what the question was really asking.

Despite having to acclimate to the language of the learning plan, learners largely find the plan helpful in developing their thinking and their projects. The following comments are indicative of the plan's benefits as related by participants.

The learning plan, even though I was confused, still made me keep going, still made me do it. It helped me put on paper what the next logical steps were in completing anything. And that's what was cool about it is because it worked for my project. It worked for Troy's project. It worked for everyone's project, and it was pretty much laid out to where as long as you did the learning plan activities, you had in your mind, you were on the right track. It did a good job of breaking things down from one big picture into small, little pictures, or anyway steps to help you reach your ultimate goal, which seemed daunting at the beginning. You couldn't really get too far off course.

I really liked it. From the beginning you asked us questions. What is, generally what is our goal, what we need to do, how many hours it's going to take approximately, what kind of machinery we are going to use and which kind of devices or whatever. The whole thing is wonderful.

One of the most important activities during staff development sessions is work on the learning plan. It is the plan that methodically guides development of learners. For this reason, it is very important that the facilitator be present when learners are writing the plan and monitor individuals' responses to the prompts. While there is no correct answer for each question, failing to understand the prompts may lead one off course and generate unnecessary frustration.

In addition to becoming comfortable with the learning plan, time is a concern for most participants. Many state that just attending sessions takes time they could use for other purposes. The benefit offered by the program is described as an off-setting factor.

For every teacher time is an issue, so to take on something else, at first, was like, I don't want to take on anything else. It's like I can't do any more, anything else.

That's when you said you can take something you want to learn and go with that. I said o.k., I'll go with trying to do the Power-Point, because I know I want to do it. I need to do something like that. It's been helpful for me, because it's made me do something I've been putting off all year.

While participating in the program, time repeatedly arises as a concern. Individuals have a strong need to use time wisely. Regularly, comments regarding mental and physical time spent on projects outside sessions are shared during group and individual reflections.

Frustration again. Waiting again. Sitting here waiting. And I'm waiting, and waiting, and waiting. I want some motion clips. I went through this once already, and the one I picked didn't move.

I've been spending time outside of class trying to schedule computer lab time, scheduling technology specialists, and requesting specialty equipment.

I've done both mental and physical work outside the staff development sessions. Mentally it just comes to mind every now and then; physically, I've interviewed other teachers on my own concerning this, which I could not do during staff development.

I'm going to sleep and waking up thinking about this damn formula.

For the facilitator, comments regarding time may become bothersome. It is helpful to remember that educators everywhere have a preoccupation with time. For most people, there simply is not enough time to do all the things they would like to do. For the facilitator, the best course of action is simply to allow group members to express their frustration regarding this issue.

A situation may, indeed, arise in which a few participants are not using their time wisely, and thus project completion is in danger. For these individuals, the facilitator should guide problem solving to address the issue. Courses of action may include revising the project if the goal was too grand to be completed in the time frame or helping the learner revisit the time frame originally established. In any case, the facilitator's role is to assist the participants in getting back on track to their goals.

CONCLUSION

Patterns of traditional staff development permeate learners' conceptions of how the program will operate. Due to the expectation they will be told exactly what to do, participants are initially cautious to accept self-direction. After the first few sessions, though, individuals begin taking ownership of their learning.

As participants face the challenges of completing their projects, emotional responses are highly common. Individuals' emotions provide an almost barometer-like reading of the degree to which they have measured up to the standards they set for themselves. The perception of others' progress, while subjective, often feeds a sense of progress or a feeling of inadequacy. On the whole, though, by the conclusion of the program all participants feel a sense of empowerment and satisfaction their needs have been met. Their thoughts about the program are largely positive, although some struggle with the learning plan and time required to attend sessions.

11

Guiding Self-Directed Learning

Do's and Don'ts

As you prepare to develop your own individualized staff development program, there are several do's and don'ts to consider. These items were covered in the preceding chapters, and they are reviewed here as a final reminder of their importance. First, structural concerns are addressed, then facilitator behaviors follow. Each concept will be presented in a graphic suggesting the "do" and "do not." After the graphic, an accompanying rationale will be provided.

STRUCTURAL CONCERNS

The structural concerns revisited here relate to planning of sessions, providing support with the learning plan, and incorporating reflection. These reminders are meant to stress the importance of each issue addressed.

DO	DO NOT
Plan sessions across time	Plan sessions back to back across a few days or a week

If the goal of the individualized staff development program was simply to have learners complete a project, that goal could certainly be accomplished across several sequential days with careful planning.

Beyond simply completing the project, though, is the goal of developing participants as self-directed, professional learners. In order for individuals to truly grow as learners, they need time to gather information, consider it in the context of their roles, reflect on it independently and with others, and apply it in legitimate situations. That process simply takes time, and it cannot be forced.

Besides the individual growth process, the larger school and district goals have to be considered as well. In order for educators to develop meaningful plans to address school-level initiatives, they must be given at least enough time to develop the plans and initially test them out. Preferably, they would be given sufficient time to determine the effectiveness of the plans and reflect upon further actions. Inarguably, opportunities to embed learning in one's role can be truly provided only across several weeks or months.

DO	DO NOT
Provide individual work time of at least 90 minutes during each session	Provide less than an hour of individual work time during each session

The staff development model described in this book was designed on one account to address participants' need for time to work on projects. Ample amounts of individual work time must be provided for learners to become engaged in and process learning. During a 90-minute span, on-task individuals can settle into mental activity and complete "chunks" of their projects fairly easily. If less than an hour is provided for independent work, individuals are forced to complete projects on their own time, creating a demand on the already limited hours they have. While participant should feel free to work on their projects outside of the sessions, it shou' be *clearly communicated* that outside work is not required as part of the p gram. Key to that communication is provision of time to meet demand the program during scheduled sessions.

DO	DO NOT
Provide support with learning plan	Leave learners to complete the learning plans on thei

The learning plan creates a framework for participants to learning. Its prompts generate planning and reflective tho' completion of the plan will lead individuals to complete t' grow professionally. Some learners, though, will have diff plan. My experience has been that almost everyone can wr the prompts, but the response may not be on target wi' asked. When learners do not quite comprehend what prompts are asking, they are unable to truly benefit from the guidance provided in the plan. In order to guide appropriate learner planning, support *must* be provided by a facilitator.

DO	DO NOT
Revisit the learning plan across sessions	Visit the learning plan at only initial and closing session activities

A good deal of the learning plan will be completed in the first few staff development sessions. The initial planning focuses learners on a goal, has them generate a timeline for completing the project, and leads them to delineate steps for completing the project. Because most of the planning has been completed early on, it may be easy to forget about the remainder of the plan.

Be certain to routinely include time during all or almost all sessions to revisit the learning plan. Completion of the plan across sessions layers reflection on learning and provides for adjustment of projects to account for learned information. As well, later prompts guide implementation of learning and evaluation of projects. Processing of information throughout the program leads to deeper, more meaningful learning, and subsequently to greater professional growth of participants.

DO	DO NOT
Incorporate individual and group reflection	Forgo cognitive processing generated by prompted reflection

For some participants, the benefits of reflection are not immediately obvious. To be certain, though, written and verbal reflections prompt cognitive processing. Both individual and group reflections were designed into the model due to the different functions they serve. As an opening activity, one provides for "cranking" thought processes, and as a closing activity, the other provides for summarily processing the day's learning. Each serves a clear purpose.

The purpose of group reflections is to engender peer support and generate thought processes associated with social interaction. The mere necessity of having to report successes, challenges, and the day's plan to the group requires one to analyze experiences, analyze how they have impacted progress, and commit to an agenda. This is done as an opening activity to refresh thinking about projects and activate a climate of social support.

Individual reflections are completed at the close of sessions to allow learners' processing of the day's experiences. In the same way the group reflection opens cognitive processing, individual reflections provide for summary processing. This reflection is written and provides a safe outlet for expressing concerns, thoughts, and questions. Facilitators are to read and respond orally to reflections during the next session, as appropriate, on an individual or group basis, but largely these reflections are to draw learner thought to a concluding place for the day.

Summary

In order to provide for individual growth, learners must have time for deep mental engagement and the support necessary to urge them along in the process. Sufficient time must be provided in each session for individual work. As well, the learning plan is integral in guiding learner thought and actions and should be revisited across sessions. Group and individual reflections draw participants to cognitively process their learning and experiences and therefore arrive at a deeper understanding of that which they are studying. Each of these components is necessary for a well-rounded self-directed program.

FACILITATOR BEHAVIORS

The facilitators will make or break the program for participants, the school, and the district. Their background knowledge and skills, as well as their ability to support adult learners, are critical to success of all involved in self-directed learning. The following are parting reminders for facilitators.

DO	DO NOT
Develop an understanding of adult learners' needs	Assume to understand adult learners' needs

Many trainers who work with educators have a K–12 teaching background. Often they make the assumption that instructional practices used with children transfer to training of adults. The best practices applied in a highly interactive classroom do transfer, but the clientele is quite different. Adult learners are motivated to learn by needs or interests, they want to be in control of their learning, they prefer hands-on learning, they desire opportunities for professional discourse with peers, they expect respect for the experience they bring, and they want to use tomorrow what they learn today.

It is critical to remember that adults should be treated with the respect accorded their age and experience. Like any other social situation, there will be individuals who are slow to understand or who behave immaturely. It is best to deal with these people in a manner that does not belittle them or mirror their inappropriate actions.

The individualized staff development program is inherently designed to address needs of adult learners. Session activities were created to address social and academic needs, but central to implementation of the program is a capable facilitator. With a little study, an understanding of adult learning is reasonably easy to develop.

DO	DO NOT
Develop an understanding of qualitative and quantitative assessments and data	Forgo developing a clear understanding of concepts central to goal development and evaluation

In order to set goals, gather data, and evaluate progress, learners will utilize various forms of data. Some participants come to the program with a basic knowledge of quantitative data, especially as they relate to averages or standardized test scores. Beyond that level, most do not have experience or understanding relating to more advanced assessment construction or data analysis. Therefore, many participants will need assistance in understanding research they may read or in formulating a method to assess their own growth or that of students.

Certainly the program is not intended to develop statisticians, nor is the facilitator required to be one. It is important, though, that the facilitator be comfortable guiding use of assessments and in analyzing both qualitative and quantitative data. Proficiency in this skill set is necessary so that adequate support can be provided to participants in information gathering, goal setting, and project evaluation. Facilitator strength in this area is very important.

DO	DO NOT
Prepare materials in advance of program commencement	Piecemeal materials on a weekly basis or attempt to run sessions "on the fly"

Organization of materials and sessions goes a long way to prepare participants themselves to be organized. It helps greatly to have ready a three-ring binder with all materials for participants when they arrive for the first session. Of particular importance are the complete learning plan and daily agendas for each session. Group members will generally complete the learning plan on the same schedule, but a few may actually advance before the rest of the group. Materials should be present to allow for this. In addition, the daily agendas allow learners to prepare in advance for the day's activities and aid the facilitator with smoother transitions. When learners are unaware of what will be next in the series of activities, they wait to be told and often lose time that could be spent engaged in learning.

While it is not absolutely critical to have all mini-lesson materials and journal pages prepared by the first session, I found that by doing so

I reduced time spent on unnecessary procedural tasks during later sessions. When materials are already bound and distributed in the binder, the sole task left to begin activities is direction to a particular section and page. Otherwise, a good 5 to 10 minutes is spent handing out pages and explaining where to place them in the binder.

Last, due to the number of activities to be conducted during any one session, it is of particular importance to have a set agenda prepared in advance of each session. While it may seem easy enough to stay on track when activities occur on a fairly routine schedule, even a brief off-task foray can deprive the group of valuable time for information processing and individual work time. The facilitator should be prepared to guide group reflection, learning plan work, mini-lessons, independent work time, and individual reflections on a specific schedule. It is even better when all participants have their own copies of the agenda so that they can aid in effectively transitioning from one activity to the next.

DO	DO NOT
Remain in a facilitative role	Take on the role of instructor

The single most important act of the facilitator is to remain in the facilitative role. To take on the role of instructor usurps learner control and reinforces the conception that there is indeed a desired project and format for learning. Remaining in the facilitative role includes empowering learners to make their own choices as to what will be learned, how it will be learned, and how results will be evaluated. As previously discussed, providing feedback regarding learner choices is certainly fine, especially when individuals are learning to set goals aligned with school and district initiatives and to determine methods for evaluating progress. Simply put, the most powerful facilitators guide learner decision making without endorsing one choice or another.

DO	DO NOT
Provide instructional guidance that helps learners stay on track	Withhold minor instructional supports that will help learners advance

While facilitators should not take on the role of instructor, they should not withhold minor supports that could help a learner advance. An example of this particular situation occurred when a retired administrator returned to the classroom. He wanted to develop his knowledge and command of spreadsheets to gather discipline data, but he had no prior exposure whatsoever to spreadsheet programs. He did not even know how to open the program already installed on his computer.

He read an instruction manual and finally opened the program a few sessions later. After about three sessions, he was becoming increasingly angry that he had not advanced in his understanding and use of spreadsheets. I decided to address his frustration by offering a brief demonstration. He accepted, and after a 10-minute tutorial, he was able to enter data. During the next session, he asked for another tutorial on making graphs. I obliged with another brief demonstration. After these minor supports, he was able to manipulate the spreadsheet and analyze data—his ultimate goal.

The distinction between facilitating and instructing is the degree of control taken from the learner. In the situation with the spreadsheet program, the learner was given just enough support to become independent. Further, that support was offered and not imposed. Critical to learners' growth is their conception that they are independently achieving success, and with too much facilitator input that perception is jeopardized.

The same concept of limited instructional support applies to individuals who request more facilitator involvement. Usually those learners who appear reluctant to take ownership after a couple of sessions are afraid of failure and therefore attempt to draw input from the facilitator. The best course of action is to assist the individuals to weigh choices and assure them that whatever choice they make can be adjusted if necessary. Again, give only as much instructional support as is necessary to help them become independent.

DO	DO NOT
Respond appropriately to learner hesitance and emotionality	Patronize or become visibly frustrated with learners

For learners, experiencing a variety of emotions is a natural outcome of the self-directed process. Even the most professional of individuals may find him- or herself uncharacteristically blowing off steam one minute and singing "Hallelujah" the next. Facilitators should understand and expect this behavior. As well, they should be highly aware of the reactions they display to particular individuals and the group in response.

Dealing with exasperated, frustrated, angry, or hesitant adults can be quite uncomfortable, and these situations can occasionally produce the same kinds of emotions for the facilitator. Sometimes it is difficult to decide whether to sit quietly and acknowledge the learner's emotions with eye contact or to do something to alleviate the tension. And there is no simple answer, as responses depend on the individuals involved and the causes behind their feelings. Regardless of the response appropriate to the situation, the facilitator should always react in a professional way that acknowledges the learner's frustration and connotes respect for the individual as an adult. Carefully measured facilitator behavior will ensure that neither the group as a whole, nor any of its members, feel patronized, disrespected, or reprimanded for the emotional responses they have.

More often than not, learners' frustrations are in response to their own perceptions they have not progressed adequately enough. Facilitator questioning is often enough to help individuals identify steps necessary to meet the expectations they have set for themselves. At the very least, the facilitator is providing a productive outlet for the participant. Some individuals may simply need a helping hand from the facilitator to overcome a barrier to progress. And there are times when people need merely to "vent" their frustrations. To the extent that affective supports do not impact other participants and do not extend beyond a reasonable amount of time, the facilitator should provide an understanding ear.

Summary

Before leading self-directed learning, facilitators should develop a firm understanding of adult learning, as the program is designed to meet this group's developmental needs. Further, it is necessary that facilitators have a clear command of basic qualitative and quantitative assessments and data. They should prepare materials in advance of implementing programs and remain in a facilitative role during program sessions. It is of utmost importance that facilitators respond appropriately to learner emotionality and provide learners guidance in staying on track toward goals.

CONCLUSION

In order to maintain the benefits of the program, there are several structural concerns and facilitator behaviors that should be accounted for in an individualized staff development program. Sessions should be planned across time, provide at least 90 minutes of independent work time, include learner support with the learning plan, provide for revisiting the learning plan across sessions, and incorporate group and individual reflections to prompt cognitive processing. Capable facilitators will develop an understanding of adult learners' needs, develop a command of qualitative and quantitative assessment and analysis, prepare session materials in advance, remain in the facilitative role, provide minor instructional supports as needed, and respond appropriately to learner hesitance and emotionality. Retaining conceptual aspects of the model should lead to a successful self-directed professional development program.

Conclusion

We have come to a time and place in the evolution of professional development for educators where it is not only essential that we address both individual teachers' needs and organizational needs, in addition to student needs, but where we are also equipped to do so. What we have learned about staff training continually reiterates the effectiveness of job-embedded learning in advancing teacher knowledge and skill, while elevating professional practice within schools. Through carefully crafted, high quality, individualized development programs, it is possible to motivate teachers to willingly confront instructional change in both their classrooms and schools.

The power behind the individualized professional development model is that it allows for the marriage of teacher needs and school goals into a single action aimed at improved student achievement. Through use of the learning plan, individual teachers develop their knowledge and skill as they see fit within the range of concerns most critical to the school. Without the prohibitive expense of hiring endless consultants and experts, administrators and staff developers can plan a top-notch, research-based training program using the greatest resource they already have—teachers.

Student achievement can be addressed at levels as broad or refined as desired in each school. Building leaders simply determine improvement focus, and teachers craft their own growth accordingly. Effectively, all parties get what they need.

Structural components of the staff development program can be easily altered in response to the state mandates, goals, resources, and philosophical approach of each organization. Staff developers are encouraged to adjust the program to meet the unique needs of those they serve. Further, they are urged to continually refine implementation procedures to address things learned during each successive run.

The intent of this book was to provide a framework for ensuring individual teachers' professional learning needs are met in an ongoing, developmentally appropriate manner. What is known about adult learning theory was combined with staff development practices effective in improving student achievement, and a method of accountability for learning was specifically designed into the program. The difficulty in meeting teachers' individual needs until now has been the availability of programs focused upon such an end. That crack has finally been sealed.

Resource A

Session Agendas

SELF-DIRECTED STAFF DEVELOPMENT PROGRAM

Session   **Activities**

I

1. Introductions, climate setting

2. In small groups, discuss: job duties, school goals, interest or growth areas. Write responses on chart paper to be shared with the group.

3. Share group responses.

4. Individual work time: Learners will complete the Worksheet for Stating Learning Objectives. In participant's notebook, each learner will complete the Responsibilities section of the learning plan.

5. Facilitator: Briefly share background, concept, and structure of self-directed learning and action research. Goal of staff development is to prepare participants to self-direct their learning. Course will be divided into two components: developing knowledge and skill as critical learners, and systematically applying knowledge and skill in a self-directed learning project.

6. Reflect in a written journal entry on thoughts/perceptions about the staff development experience.

Assignment for next session: Select a learning goal and think about how to achieve it. Bring materials for work time.

II

1. In small groups, discuss learning goal and how it might be achieved.

2. Briefly, individuals share their goals with the whole group.

3. Individual work time: Work on learning plan. Complete Identifying Focus, Defining the Problem, Planning for Self-Directed Study, and the Research/Data Gathering section of Self-Directed Study. Work on project for remainder of time.

4. Facilitator: Share and explain template for evaluating written material.

5. Reflect in a written journal entry on thoughts/perceptions about the staff development experience.

Assignment for next session: Determine baseline levels of knowledge/skill/performance you wish to change (pre-project assessment). Bring materials for work time.

III

1. In whole group, discuss concerns, comments, pre-project assessment, status.

2. Arrange in project groups according to similar learning projects. These groups will remain intact for the remainder of sessions. Groups are to serve as supportive friends in meeting project goal. In small groups, discuss pre-project assessment and its implications. Work on learning plan. Complete the Pre-Project Assessment and Summary/Interpretation of Pre-Project Assessment sections of Self-Directed Study.

3. Facilitator: Present lesson on critically evaluating information. What kind of information is it? Who is presenting it? If it is research, what kind is it? If not research, is it based upon research? If not, what makes you comfortable you can trust the information?

4. Facilitator: Demonstrate how to use an online database for locating information.

5. Individual work time: Work on project.

6. Reflect in a written journal entry on thoughts/perceptions about the staff development experience.

Assignment for next session: Bring materials for work time.

IV

1. With the whole group, briefly share progress.

2. In project group, discuss progress and concerns in more detail.

3. Facilitator: Present basic terminology of quantitative and qualitative research.

4. Individual work time: Work on project.

5. Reflect in a written journal entry on thoughts/perceptions about the staff development experience.

Assignment for next time: Think about how you will translate what you are learning to a plan of action. Bring materials for work time.

V

1. In project group, discuss implications of learning to date and how they relate to goal.

2. Facilitator: How will new knowledge be transferred to an action plan?

   What actions are most likely to contribute to goal attainment? (Select 1–3 actions.)

   For each action, how will a successful outcome look?

   How will success of each action be assessed?

   List steps and time frame for implementing each action.

   What materials, supplies, or personnel are required to implement the action plan?

3. Work on learning plan. Complete Interpretation of Research/Data Gathering and Translating New Knowledge/Skills Into Plan to Meet Goals sections of Self-Directed Learning.

4. Individual work time: Work on projects.

5. Reflect in a written journal entry on thoughts/perceptions about the staff development experience.

Assignment for next session: Think about how you might/try to implement your action plan over the next few weeks. Bring materials to work.

VI

1. In project group, discuss action plans and concerns.

2. In large group, briefly share action plans and present concerns to group.

3. Facilitator: Solicit brainstorming and discuss types of things to observe in classroom—related to implementing action plan, as a variety of variables (e.g., traffic flow, behavioral patterns, student affect, ability levels, etc.) might have an impact on effectiveness.

4. Individual work time: Work on project.

5. Reflect in a written journal entry on thoughts/perceptions about the staff development experience.

Assignment for next session: As you reflect upon/implement your action plan, are there any modifications you may need to make to the original plan? Bring materials to work on individual project.

VII

1. In project group, discuss progress, concerns, and any modifications to original action plan.

2. In large group, briefly share progress, concerns, and modifications to action plan.

3. Facilitator: Discuss reflecting on actions taken and results of action. The key point is that learning is a dynamic process that calls for alteration of behavior as new information is gained.

4. Work on learning plan. Complete the Implementation of Plan to Meet Goals section of Self-Directed Learning.

5. Individual work time: Work on project.

6. Reflect in a written journal entry on thoughts/perceptions about the staff development experience.

Assignment for next session: Be ready to do a 5- to 10-minute presentation to the whole group on your project.

VIII

1. In participant's notebook, work on learning plan. Complete the Post-Project Assessment and Summary/Interpretation of Post-Project Assessment sections of Self-Directed Learning.

2. Organize thoughts, materials for 5- to 10-minute presentation. Discuss presentation plan with project group for last-minute suggestions.

3. Present projects to whole group.

4. Reflect in a written journal entry on thoughts/perceptions about the staff development experience.

Resource B

Learning Plan

Name _____ Date _____

Position _____

Responsibilities

Organizational Goals

School

District

Instruction

Administration

Management/Discipline

Other

Identifying Focus

Area of interest or targeted change/improvement

Reason for interest/concern regarding this area

How does this interest/concern relate to your responsibilities?

Describe how development in this area will improve student achievement. Include background data regarding this area. Describe student achievement outcomes that can be verified by data.

How does this relate to schoolwide and systemwide goals?

Defining the Problem

List the goals you hope to accomplish as a result of developing your knowledge and skills in the focus area. Phrase the outcomes as observable behaviors.

Identify the process(es) you will use to assess *your* pre- and post-project levels of performance, behavior, thinking, understanding, and so on. Be certain these assessments correlate with the outcomes you hope to achieve as a result of study in the focus area.

Identify indicators of success that demonstrate achievement of study goals.

Identify the methods you will use to demonstrate the impact of your study on student achievement. What data will you collect to measure change?

Planning for Self-Directed Study

Mode for conducting study

☐ Self-instruction

☐ Cooperative Learning (Group study)

Group members _____

☐ Team Learning (Group study for core material and self-instruction for corollary info)

Group members _____

☐ Other _____

What organizational method will you utilize to organize your data and resources?

☐ Three-ring binder or portfolio   ☐ Spiral notebook/journal

☐ Folders/filing system   ☐ Multimedia

☐ Electronic format   ☐ Other _____

Define the time frame in which you plan to complete the project.

_____

_____

_____

Entire Project:

_____

_____

_____

Project Components:

_____

_____

_____

Pre-project assessment _____

_____

Summary/interpretation of pre-project assessment _____

_____

Research/data gathering _____

_____

Interpretation of research/data gathering _____

_____

Translating new knowledge/skills into plan to meet goals _____

_____

Implementation of plan to meet goals _____

_____

Post-project assessment _____

_____

Summary/interpretation of post-study assessment _____

_____

SELF-DIRECTED STUDY

Research/Data Gathering

List topics and key words to be utilized in study of your focus area.

_____

_____

_____

_____

_____

_____

Methods you will utilize to gather information about your focus area.

☐ Magazine and journal articles   ☐ Online research

☐ Professional books   ☐ Multimedia
                                       (video, tape recording, etc.)

☐ Other professional documents   ☐ Expert sources

☐ Interviews/surveys   ☐ Others' observation of me

☐ Observation of others   ☐ Other _____

In gathering information about my focus area, I may need help with:

Pre-Project Assessment

List results of pre-study assessment.

_____

_____

_____

_____

_____

_____

Summary/Interpretation of Pre-Project Assessment

Summarize the implications of pre-study assessment.

_____

_____

_____

_____

_____

Did the results of the pre-study assessment validate or alter the focus of your interest or concern? Briefly explain.

_____

_____

_____

_____

_____

_____

_____

Is it necessary to refine your area of interest or concern. If yes, how will you modify your project?

_____

_____

_____

_____

_____

_____

Interpretation of Research/Data Gathering

Summarize the most significant findings of your research/data gathering as they relate to your focus area. (What important points do the data reveal? What patterns or trends are noted? How do data from various sources compare and contrast? Do any correlations seem important?)

_____

_____

_____

_____

_____

_____

Discuss your inferences/feelings/opinions regarding the data you have gathered. (Are the results different from what you expected? Did the data validate or alter your focus area? How did the data impact your thinking regarding the focus area?)

_____

_____

_____

_____

_____

_____

Translating New Knowledge/ Skills Into Plan to Meet Goals

Discuss the implications of your research/data gathering as they relate to your goal and student achievement. (What must you consider as you design a plan for meeting your goal and addressing your responsibilities?)

_____

_____

_____

_____

_____

Identify actions most likely to contribute to goal attainment and improved student achievement. (Focus on one to three strategies, innovations, or changes.)

_____

_____

_____

_____

_____

_____

_____

For each action listed above, describe how a successful outcome will look.

_____

_____

_____

_____

_____

_____

Describe in detail how you will assess the success of each action. Be certain that the assessment and action are compatible, and that both directly relate to your focus area. When appropriate, include copies of any surveys, interview questions, or other assessments. If applicable, provide a description of statistics you will collect, and explain how these can indicate success.

_____

_____

_____

_____

_____

For each action, list steps required for implementation and provide a time frame for implementing each step. If the time frame for a step may vary, indicate the criteria that will be used to mark conclusion of the step.

_____

_____

_____

_____

_____

_____

List materials, supplies, or personnel required to implement your action plan.

_____

_____

_____

_____

_____

_____

Implementation of Plan to Meet Goals

List the actions taken and their accompanying steps. For each step, note comments, results, or other pertinent information relating to the implementation of your action plan. Include any deviations from the plan and reasons for the change.

_____

_____

_____

_____

_____

_____

_____

List your response/opinion/feelings regarding the action plan(s). Did the process occur as you had envisioned it? Why or why not? What information did you gain? Are there steps you would eliminate, add, or alter?

_____

_____

_____

_____

_____

_____

_____

Post-Project Assessment

Discuss the design of your post-project assessment. Did you utilize the method you originally planned? If not, why did you select a different measure, and how does it compare to the pre-project assessment you conducted?

_____

_____

_____

_____

_____

_____

Describe the results of your post-project assessment, focusing on outcomes you had hoped to achieve and indicators of success identified at the outset of your project.

_____

_____

_____

_____

_____

_____

Summary/Interpretation of Post-Project Assessment

Based upon the results of post-study assessment of your growth, did you reach the outcomes you hoped to achieve as a result of study in the focus area? Explain.

_____

_____

_____

_____

_____

_____

Describe progress in relation to indicators of success identified at the outset of the study. What degree of progress was made in relation to these indicators? After concluding your development in the focus area, do you feel the indicators identified are appropriate measures of success?

_____

_____

_____

_____

_____

_____

Discuss the implications of your results.

_____

_____

_____

_____

_____

_____

As a result of your development in the focus area, what further inter-est areas, questions, or growth opportunities have you identified?

_____

_____

_____

_____

_____

_____

_____

Summarize the impact of development in the focus area on your ability to carry out your responsibilities. Discuss how student achievement was impacted. Describe results of collected data.

_____

_____

_____

_____

_____

_____

_____

Resource C

Reproducible Templates

Worksheet for Stating Learning Objectives

Behavioral Aspect	Topics for Study	Background Student Achievement Data/Rationale for Interest
I want to develop my *knowledge* about:	1. 2. 3. 4. 5. 6. 7.	
I would like to better *understand:*	1. 2. 3. 4. 5. 6. 7.	
I want to develop *skill* in:	1. 2. 3. 4. 5. 6. 7.	
I would like to *develop or create:*	1. 2. 3. 4. 5. 6. 7.	
I would like to develop *an appreciation or value* of:	1. 2. 3. 4. 5. 6. 7.	

SOURCE: Adapted from Knowles (1975).

EVALUATING WRITTEN MATERIAL

TITLE:

AUTHOR:

SOURCE:

DATE/VOLUME/ISSUE:

TYPE: Research-Quantitative   Research-Qualitative   Not Research

Book   Journal Article   Newspaper Article   Web Info.

Other_____

Topic:

Summary:

Implications for Project:

SOURCE: Adapted from Calhoun (1994).

TEST DATA INTERPRETATION WORKSHEET

Directions: Using the scale at the top of the page, place a mark on the bottom portion of the worksheet in the place that best represents each student score. By the mark, write the numeric score, what the score represents, and the test name. After all information has been transferred to the worksheet, analyze trends in the data.

SS		70		85		100		115	130
%ile	10	20	30	40	50	60	70	80	90
Stanine	1		3		5		7		9

Significantly Below Average   Average   Above Significantly

Below Average   Above Average

Codes:

SS–Standard Score (Mean = 100), %ile–Percentile (Range 1–100, Mean = 50)

References

Acheson, K., & Gall, M. (1997). *Techniques in the clinical supervision of teachers: Preservice and inservice applications* (4th ed.). New York: John Wiley.

Auger, W., & Wideman, R. (2000). Using action research to open the door to life-long professional learning. *Education, 121,* 120–127.

Black, S. (1998). Money and the art of staff development. *Journal of Staff Development, 2,* 14–17.

Blase, J., & Blase, J. R. (1994). *Empowering teachers: What successful principals do.* Thousand Oaks, CA: Corwin Press.

Blase, J., & Blase, J. R. (1998). *Handbook of instructional leadership.* Thousand Oaks, CA: Corwin Press.

Bonham, A. (1992). Major learning efforts: Recent research and future directions. In G. J. Confessore & S. J. Confessore (Eds.), *Guideposts to self-directed learning: Expert commentary on essential concepts* (pp. 48–54). King of Prussia, PA: Organization Design and Development.

Calhoun, E. F. (1994). *How to use action research in the self-renewing school.* Alexandria, VA: Association for Supervision and Curriculum Development.

Collinson, V. (2000). Staff development by any other name: Changing words or changing practices? *Educational Forum, 64,* 124–132.

Corabi, J. (1995). A case study of professional growth programs in a local suburban school district: Personal evaluations of professional growth and the building of a professional culture. *Dissertation Abstracts International.* (UMI No. 9537082)

Craft-Tripp, M. (1993). Self-directed development for special educators: A field study of a goal-setting approach to professional development. *Dissertation Abstracts International.* (UMI No. 9317107)

Deojay, T., & Pennington, L. (2000, Winter). Reaching Heather: Three steps use data to connect staff development with student learning. *National Staff Development Council,* pp. 42–46.

Duron, D. (1994). Elementary teachers' perceptions regarding professional growth within the school setting. *Dissertation Abstracts International.* (UMI No. 9416316)

Feldman, A. (1998). Implementing and assessing the power of conversation in the teaching of action research. *Teacher Education Quarterly, 25,* 27–42.

Garrison, D. R. (1993). An analysis of the control construct in self-directed learning. In H. B. Long & Associates, *Emerging perspectives of self-directed learning* (pp. 27–43). Norman: University of Oklahoma, Oklahoma Research Center for Continuing Professional and Higher Education.

Georgia Department of Education. (1997). *Resource guide for staff development.* Atlanta, GA: Author.

Guskey, T. (1995). *Results-oriented professional development: In search of an optimal mix of effective practices.* North Central Regional Educational Laboratory. Retrieved March 17, 2001, from www.ncrel.org/sdrs/areas/rpl_esys/pdlitrev.htm

Hirsch, S., & Sparks, D. (1999). Helping teachers grow. *American School Board Journal, 186,* 37–40.

Husby, V. (2002). *Teachers' perspectives on a self-directed staff development program based upon principles of action research,* Unpublished doctoral dissertation, University of Georgia.

Jensen, E. (1996). *Brain-based learning.* Del Mar, CA: Turning Point.

Kasworm, C. E. (1992). The adult's learning projects: A fresh approach to theory and practice in adult learning. In G. J. Confessore & S. J. Confessore (Eds.), *Guideposts to self-directed learning: Expert commentary on essential concepts* (2nd ed., pp. 55–73). King of Prussia, PA: Organization Design and Development.

Knowles, M. (1975). *Self-directed learning: A guide for learners and teachers.* Englewood, CA: Cambridge Adult Education.

Knowles, M. S. (1989). *The making of an adult educator: An autobiographical journey.* San Francisco: Jossey-Bass.

Knowles, M. S., Holton, E. F., & Swanson, R. A. (1998). *The adult learner: The definitive classic in adult education and human resources development* (5th ed.). Houston, TX: Butterworth-Heinemann.

Lindeman, E. C. (1926). *The meaning of adult education.* New York: New Republic. Retrieved July 15, 2001, from www.infed.org/archives/e-texts/lindem1.htm

Long, H. B. & Associates. (1993). *Emerging perspectives of self-directed learning.* Norman: University of Oklahoma, Oklahoma Research Center for Continuing Professional and Higher Education.

MacMillan, R. B. (1999). Influences of workplace conditions on teachers' job satisfaction. *Journal of Educational Research, 93,* 39–47.

Mezirow, J. (2000). Learning to think like an adult. In J. Mezirow & Associates, *Learning as transformation* (pp. 3–33). San Francisco: Jossey-Bass.

Murphy, C. (1999, Spring). Use time for faculty study. *National Staff Development Council,* pp. 20–25.

National Staff Development Council. (1994). *Standards for staff development: Middle level edition.* Oxford, OH: Author.

National Staff Development Council. (2001). *Standards for staff development* (Rev. ed.). Oxford, OH: Author.

Nunley, K. (2000, April). *Keeping pace with today's quick brains.* Retrieved July 15, 2001, from www.brains.org/articles.htm

Olgren, C. H. (1993). Cognitive strategies and self-directedness: Research into adults' learning processes. In H. B. Long & Associates, *Emerging perspectives of self-directed learning* (pp. 99–115). Norman: University of Oklahoma, Oklahoma Research Center for Continuing Professional and Higher Education.

Poetter, T., McKamey, C., Ritter, C., & Tisdel, P. (1999). Emerging profiles of teacher-mentors as researchers: Benefits of shared inquiry. *Action in Teacher Education, 21,* 102–126.

Robertson, J. (2000). The three r's of action research methodology: Reciprocity, reflexivity, and reflection-on-reality. *Educational Action Research, 8,* 307–325.

Roulston, K. (2001). *Handouts for ERSH 7400: Qualitative research traditions.* Athens: University of Georgia.

Sardo-Brown, D. (1995). The action research endeavors of six classroom teachers and their perceptions of action research. *Education, 116,* 196–201.

Schnitjer, K. (1994). *Overlays for ERS 611: Applied descriptive statistics.* Athens: University of Georgia.

Sherin, M. (2000). Viewing teaching on videotape. *Educational Leadership, 57,* 36–38.

Tichenor, M., & Heins, E. (2000). Study groups: An inquiry-based approach to improving schools. *Clearing House, 6,* 316–319.

Tough, A. (1992). Foreword. In H. B. Long & Associates, *Guideposts to self-directed learning: Expert commentary on essential concepts* (pp. ix–xi). King of Prussia, PA: Organization Design and Development.

Vulliamy, G. (1991). Teacher research and education change: An empirical study. *British Educational Research Journal, 17,* 219–237.

Zeichner, K., Klehr, M., & Caro-Bruce, C. (2000, Fall). Pulling their own levers. *National Staff Development Council,* pp. 36–40.

Index